Tammy, keep Shining, Catherine

Shine On, You Crazy Diamond

Even When Your Crown Feels Heavy

Catherine L. Owens

ISBN: 978-1-7348302-3-1

The author disclaims responsibility for adverse effects or consequences from the misapplication or injudicious use of the information contained in this book. Mention of resources and associations does not imply an endorsement.

This book is dedicated to my daughter, Sabrianna, who has played the greatest role in helping me become not only the woman that I am but the woman I am still becoming. I will forever be grateful for your courage to use your voice to help me find mine again.

To my niece, Mariana, who had her voice silenced way too early, but whose light continues to shine brightly within all of us who were blessed to know her.

To my mother, Sylvia, whose strength, perseverance, and compassion for others helped show me the way so many times throughout my life.

And to my sister, Angela, who embodies *Shine On, You Crazy Diamond, Even When Your Crown Feels Heavy*, more than anyone I know.

Disclaimer

There are stories in this book that may be uncomfortable for people close to me to read. My intent in sharing certain stories is in no way meant to hurt or shed any negative light on anyone. These are moments that impacted my life and were significant in my personal journey of healing, growing, and becoming the woman and person that I am today. I struggled for a long time about whether or not to share them but staying quiet and pretending they weren't significant goes against all that this book is meant to be. This is not only for myself but for all the women who may be inspired or helped by my courage and willingness to share.

"Shine. This is your day to shine, your day to let your sparkle out into the world.
Now is the time to go towards your dreams with abandon.
Now is the time to lust towards your goals with the fire in your bones
and passion flowing through your veins.
Now is the time to nourish your mind and body and take care of your spirit.
Now is the time to celebrate all that you are
and prepare for everything that's to come.
Now is the time to let your wonderful and unique true self out.
Now is the time to let yourself shine,
my beautiful friend."

– *Walk the Earth*

Contents

Introduction

The following is an entry from my journal when I was fourteen years old, titled *My Personal Philosophy*:

I was placed here as a divine daughter of my father in heaven. I have been given a special calling in which I will strive to live worthy enough to obtain. Everything I do and say today will have an effect on the earth's course tomorrow. I will try to never intentionally do or say anything that will damage another person's spirit, for a damaged spirit is like an eagle with debris in his wings. It will be unable to soar for it will be held down.

I shall polish my strengths to help me obtain my goals in this life that I wish to reach. Along with that I will accept my failures and weaknesses and see them as a challenge and use them as a learning experience. I will not sit back and watch an opportunity to succeed pass me by. While I am here, I will maximize my potential and determination to the fullest. The average person uses only 5% of his potential. If I can just strive to use 1% more, then I will stand ahead and make a difference. I deserve the best and will never settle for anything of lower value. When the time has come to leave this earth, I will leave in peace knowing that I have done my best to accomplish all that was possible. If I have helped one person improve himself, then I know my time here will have not been wasted.

Fast forward 30 years later to another Journal entry:

Empty. Just complete emptiness. Realizing I've gone from sad, overwhelmed, and depressed, to feeling numb and almost void of emotions. I would love to cry but there aren't any tears left to cry. How did I get here? How do I get past here? How does complete exhaustion turn into not even having the ability to feel tired and worn out anymore? I have felt such loneliness in feeling as if no one really knows me. The truth is I feel as if I don't even know or recognize myself anymore. How does one go from living with intention to struggling just to live?

That second journal entry was written around the time my daughter Sabri came to me and wanted me to listen to a song called "Brave" by Sara Bareilles. She was not blind, nor were many of my family and closest friends. Honestly, how I got to the place where "I wasn't myself anymore," where I had learned the biggest lie of all, "I'm fine," was so slow and subtle that it took me a while to see it happening. I have always been the strong, positive, rise-above-any-obstacle Wonder Woman kind of girl, defending the underdog, speaking my mind, making my voice heard and my opinion count, confidently holding my head high, convinced I was worthy of and capable of accomplishing anything I set my mind to. Along with that, I have had times in my life (too many) where I have had to pick up the pieces, rise from the ashes, and rebuild my life, figuring out a way to make it happen, and at times, just survive. I was no stranger to struggle, adversity, and challenges, but this was different. This was a place where I was not familiar, where I had given up hope, completely lost my voice, staying caged up to keep the peace and not stir the pot, or heaven forbid, make anyone feel uncomfortable or accountable….

It had been a few years since I had remarried, and in the beginning, it was wonderful. We were both at similar stages in our lives, professionally and with our families and children. We had similar values and interests and could talk about anything. I had been with men that were threatened by strong, independent, successful women in the past, and I felt like I had finally found a man who wasn't—a man who supported my desire for personal growth, for sharing my talents, and my desire to leave my mark while making a difference in people's lives.

And then I got a promotion at work. This was the first time I saw his insecurities come out. Do not get me wrong—I am the first to admit I have plenty of my own insecurities. The difference was that instead of talking about them, he would say something belittling or mean and get upset with me for the most random, simple thing that was usually followed by days of the silent treatment. I spent those moments trying to figure out what the hell I had done to cause him to be so upset, mean, and withholding of affection or even simple basic communication. I remember one time I had been traveling all week for work and was exhausted by the end of the week. I crashed on Friday night and slept in until 10:00 the next morning. This was not unusual for us, but for some reason, that week, it was. It upset him so much that "I didn't care enough about him or our time together" to get up early to spend time together.

It took me many moments like this to realize it wasn't anything I had done. These moments happened every time I experienced success, received a compliment, wanted to set a goal, or improve on something—things like making a bucket list, improving my credit score, writing my first book, and getting my hair and nails done on days he had off were all things that caused him to say things such as, "I guess I care about our family more than you."

"Can't you just be happy with where you are and what you have?"

"Do I not give you enough?"

"If you are so unhappy, why don't you leave?"

I did not realize all the subtle ways he was nicking away at my self-esteem and self-worth. Instead, I just tried to convince him (and myself) that I was happy, that it was enough, that he and family came before anything else. When I had been impacted by identity theft and had my credit ruined, it was important to me to rebuild my credit. It was things like this that made him say, "Clearly, you don't need me, or you wouldn't feel like you need to rebuild your credit."

I remember thinking, "What forty-year-old doesn't want good credit when it plays a role in so many areas of one's life?" But as with other ridiculous moments like this, I decided to just keep my mouth shut. It was not worth the fight or contention it caused. The times I did try to share my thoughts or opinions or call him on his bullshit, he told me, "Clearly, the conversation is over." So,

I just stopped talking or standing up for myself. Without even realizing it, I had started down a path of slowly losing myself, slipping into this pretty little cage where I was to be seen, not heard.

From the outside looking in, we had it all. We had built the dream life—a beautiful family, good health, successful careers, accomplished, well-rounded kids, two beautiful homes, and so on. What more could a person want?

Me, I just wanted to be seen and heard. After listening to the song "Brave" (over and over) that Sabri shared with me, and a few more painful moments, I finally got the courage to tell my husband I felt we needed to go to marriage counseling—and of course, he felt we did not. Why would we? Everything was "fine." And it was, as far as he knew, because I had stopped speaking up and instead walked on eggshells for years trying to keep the peace.

He finally agreed to go. We went for a few months, with me being careful on what I said and him being the caring, confused-as-to-why-we-were-there husband. A few months in, at a session of all of us just sitting there in silence, the counselor stated, "Catherine, you seem really upset," and I found myself thinking of the lyrics to the song that my daughter had shared…

> "Maybe there's a way out of the cage where you live
> Maybe one of these days you can let the light in
> Show me how big your brave is."

And so, with my voice shaking and whole-body trembling, I said it out loud, "I am."

In that moment, everything I had been keeping tucked in, nice and neat, for no one to see or hear, was out in the open. All the things I was upset about—being silenced when I had a differing opinion, being made to feel guilty for wanting to learn and grow and stand in my light, for wanting to try new things, share my talents, speak my mind, make a difference, receiving the silent treatment and withholding of affection when I had done something to upset him, taking the blame to just make all that stop. For years of walking on eggshells. For all the times he would dote on me in public and say the most charming things when others were listening and watching, yet treat me so differently when we were alone. I went on and on, and at the end, I had to admit that I was most upset with myself—upset with myself for accepting it, for staying quiet, and not standing up for myself. For letting it all happen and for allowing myself to be treated that way.

I have come to realize that even when we are born with such an innate belief in ourselves, how easily that belief can become masked, hidden, or taken from us. I am also learning just how much of an impact environmental circumstance, the value systems of society, cultural conditioning, family expectations, religious upbringing, abuse and traumas, choices we make, the opinions of others, along with many other factors can and will influence that belief in ourselves, often hindering all we are meant to do and be. There are those life-altering, out-of-our-control, defining moments, where life as we know it will never be the same, and then there are those situations that so subtly create debris in our wings, happening so slowly over time, that we don't really notice the effects they are having on our spirit, our confidence and self-worth. Without even realizing it, we have let the influence of all those things create a belief in ourselves, of what our worth is, and what it is that defines us.

My hope in writing this book is that by sharing some personal experiences of lessons learned through the process of clearing out the debris of shame, guilt, unrealistic expectations from self and others, social stigmas, childhood traumas, and other unnecessary and unrealistic pressures that we as women often put on ourselves, that I will hopefully inspire other women to use their personal experiences, circumstances, past decisions, hurts, and disappointments, as opportunities for healing and growth, freeing themselves of the cages that keep them from believing in themselves, living a life with intention, joy, love, and purpose, where they stand in their truth and light, as they become the incredible woman that they are capable of and meant to be.

1

Behind These Castle Walls

Personal Journal Entry:

I'm fine, is really I'm tired, overwhelmed, frustrated, scared, lonely, confused, discouraged, and sad. I wish I were able to share that without feeling like I was going to disappoint people. I wish I could feel all of this without disappointing myself. How do I learn to let someone love me despite my flaws, imperfections, and weaknesses when I can't even love them myself? How do I learn to redefine my expectations of perfection? Why am I so giving and patient with others, yet have no patience with myself or allow others to give in return? Why do I believe we are all worthy of unconditional love, yet I am convinced it's only certain conditions that make me worthy of love? Why do I want so badly for someone to truly know me, yet I close myself off from anyone who tries? Strength, perfectionism, high standards, keeping emotions to myself, have all served me so well throughout my life and they have also hindered me in areas of my life.

I want to scream, cry, breakdown and let it all out without feeling weak, like a failure. I want someone to say it's okay, you've been strong long enough. I want someone, just for a moment, to be strong for me instead of me always being the strong one. I want someone to see me, the real me, enough to know that I need that…

I remember telling my marriage counselor what a strange and lonely place it was to wake up one day and realize that not only do you not know yourself anymore, but everyone around you doesn't really know the real you or what it is you're going through. A lot of that was due to all the coping mechanisms I had learned throughout my life. I had the unrealistic idea that if I didn't have it all together, I was failing, if I admitted I was struggling, I was weak, and if I was not perfect in every way, I was not worthy of acceptance and love.

She encouraged me to find a few women that I felt comfortable around and let down some of my walls with them. Let them get to know and see not only the strong, independent, professional, composed, perfectly put together me, but the sensitive, hurting, confused, and overwhelmed me. Right—let down some of my walls. Those walls that had been so meticulously designed and constructed over the years for self-protection and personal survival. Right…

But I was committed to doing whatever it took to get back to me, so I did as she had suggested, and I slowly, and very cautiously, let a few women in. I wasn't quite ready to tear down the walls, but I did open a few windows and shared some of the struggles I was going through. And what happened was exactly what my counselor knew would happen. I learned I was not alone, that they too had struggles they were working through that no one really knew about, even the ones I thought had it all together. It made me realize how often we really have no idea what others are going through, that we as women often feel we need to put on the smile and say, "I'm fine" when we really aren't, all to play the role of being strong and having it all together, even on the days when just getting out of bed takes all the strength we have.

"You'd be surprised by how many times a woman sits in her car, or in the shower, or in the laundry room, or at the sink and quickly cries because she's stressed. Because when she shows her face again, she looks untouched and unbothered, manages to sport a beautiful smile, and carries on like she's fine. Women are some of the most resilient creatures. Appreciate them."

– Ravenwolf

"You will never know what someone is dealing with behind closed doors. No matter how happy someone looks, how loud their laugh is, how big their smile is, there can still be a level of hurt that is indescribable. So be kind. Even when others are not, choose to be kind."

– ANDREA RUSSETT

"We all have struggles. We all have pain. It's not a competition. I hope you are mindful enough to understand that someone else's struggle may look like a lighter load to carry, but that doesn't make it less of a struggle. It can still be just as heavy as yours. Understanding that goes a long way."

– Stephanie Bennett-Henry

"The world is full of precious souls wearing masks to hide the pain."

– Alfa

"Note to Self:

When someone is clearly not fine
and you want to tell them it's all
going to be ok or that everything
happens for a reason, stop. Just
stop. Because that is some
well intentioned, diminishing,
minimizing crap. When someone
is not ok, they're NOT ok. That's
valid. Sometimes, all people need
is to be seen and heard
and witnessed and loved."

– Nanea Hoffman

"I asked her if she was OK, and she said, 'I'm fine, I swear.'
But when I looked into her eyes, I clearly saw her struggle there.
She quickly looked away and tried her best smile.
She said softly, 'I'll make it through this; it's just taking me a while.'
I knew she was hurting, and I knew her pain was deep.
But she felt the burden was hers and hers alone to keep.
I reached out to her, and our hands intertwined.
I said, 'I love you, my friend, so your burdens are also mine.'"

– THE SHY POET

"Some people aren't good at asking for help because they're so used to being the helper. Throughout their life, they've experienced an unbalanced give and take, so their instinct is usually, 'I'll figure it out on my own.' The self-reliance is all they've ever known."

– UNKNOWN

"There are days when you have to admit that you are not okay and haven't been for a long time. And you cry it out for as long as you need to. There is nothing wrong with that."

– STEPHANIE BENNETT-HENRY

"Those eggshells you walk on to keep the peace only get louder the more you avoid why you have to walk on them in the first place.

Sweep them up, pour them in the middle of the room, and refuse to ever bend to someone else's breaking ever again. Even your own.

You are bigger than the trauma that you learn to walk around for fear you may wake a monster you know well.

Walk straight through it, babe. It is the only way."

– Stephanie Bennett-Henry

"Don't invalidate or minimalize how you feel. If you feel something, you feel it, and it's real to you. Nothing anyone says has the power to invalidate that. Ever. No one else lives in your body. No one else sees life through your eyes. No one else has lived through your experiences. And so, no one else has the right to dictate or judge how you feel. Your feelings are important, and you deserve to be heard. They are inherently valid, and they matter. Don't let anyone make you believe otherwise."

– Daniell Koepke

"There is nothing more toxic than yourself guarding your secrets, hiding your tears, silencing your screams, and destroying your soul."

– Unknown

"I've learned that not speaking on things just to keep the 'peace' is actually a trauma response. When you do this, you disrespect your boundaries. No matter what, keep taking up space with your voice."

– Unknown

"And if speaking up for myself, putting my foot down and not tolerating even a smidgen of bad treatment from you makes me 'too much to deal with' in your eyes? Then please, write those very words on a crown and hand it over to me so that I can rock the shit out of it proudly, every single day."

– Cici B.

"Women don't need to find a voice. They have a voice. They need to feel empowered to use it, and people need to be encouraged to listen."

– Megan Markle

"Just speak up. Learn to say, 'That's on you. How you move is on you. The choices you make are all on you. The way you live is all on you.' Stop absorbing the pain of other people. Recognize what belongs to you and what doesn't."

– Unknown

"Speak boldly with intellect. Never hush your voice for someone's comfort. Speak your mind, make people uncomfortable."

– Unknown

"One of the most beautiful sounds that I've ever heard is the sound of a beautiful, strong woman's voice once she has discovered her true words. She sounds empowered, she sounds confident, but most of all, she sounds free."

– Unknown

"When you are brave, you empower others around you to be brave too."

– Unknown

"So as you think about how to raise your daughter to be a confident and courageous woman, sure of herself and resilient under pressure, begin by considering where you need to practice a little more bravery yourself. Anytime you tiptoe around an awkward conversation, allow someone to treat you poorly, avoid taking a risk for fear of failure or let other people's opinions matter more than your own, you're missing an important opportunity to teach your daughter how to be brave."

– Margie Warrell

"The era of sweeping shit under the rug is over. Folks need to be uncomfortable."

– UNKNOWN

"It's OK, girl. You just forgot who you are. Welcome back."

– UNKNOWN

2

We All Live in a Cage with the Door Wide Open

I will never forget the simple yet profound feeling I had as I sat on my bed, on the phone with my ex-husband, and told him I wanted a divorce, that I needed to get back to "me." As the words slipped off my tongue, all I thought was, *I feel like a bird that has escaped her cage….*

I sat there thinking of all the times in life, without realizing it, that we allow our wings to get clipped or held down. Whether it's a bad relationship, a toxic home or work environment, addiction, low self-esteem, unrealistic expectations, and pressures that we put on ourselves because of others' wants and needs, social and religious beliefs, along with many things we let define who we are and the life we are supposed to live. And why we often struggle and feel guilty for being true to who we are, especially when it goes against all we have been taught or come to believe is right or wrong, good or bad, acceptable or unacceptable, success or failure. All those things we allow to keep us caged from soaring and discovering just how high and far we can go when we are living a life that is true to who we are and what we want, need, and desire.

What other cages was I allowing myself to live in and why?

What cages are you allowing yourself to live in and why?

"There is freedom waiting for you on the breezes of the sky. And you ask, what if I fall? Oh, but darling, what if you fly?"

– UNKNOWN

"You can't keep her in a cage, clip her wings, tell her lies, say that fragile birds were never meant to fly. Watch her live behind a rusted door, latched tight, her spirit slipping away so you can keep her inside. Beautiful creatures cannot be confined. Her wings will grow; she'll find the sky."

– Christy Ann Martine

"They say it happens. It builds up… it boils over. You reach your limit, and you snap. Everyone around you thinks it happened in an instant. A split decision. But it is nothing of the sort. It happens when your self-worth suddenly bitch slaps your fear. And it's a beautiful thing to watch a person 'snap' into the person that is deserving of life."

– ALFA

"Don't tell a girl with fire in her veins and hurricane bones what she should and shouldn't do. In the blink of an eye, she will shatter that ridiculous cage you attempt to build around her beautiful bohemian spirit."

– Melody Lee

"She was a free spirit guided by the wind, and nobody could tell her how to live because of the fire in her heart and the passion in her eyes. She was like a bird who had never been caged and never would be."

– MARC ANTHONY

"I was never meant to be kept in a cage or anything that resembles one. I was never meant to be trapped or enslaved by anything, including my fears or my addictions. I am not just meant to fly… I am meant to soar. I must remember to never let anything enslave me. My life is too important. I am a brave girl. I was born to fly free."

– Unknown

"You were born with potential.
You were born with goodness and trust.
You were born with ideals and dreams.
You were born with wings.
You are not meant for crawling, so don't.
You have wings.
Learn to use them and fly."

– Rumi

Survivor
"We are not barbarians.
We are contained ferocity.
What happens when you
keep something caged
and limit its ability to fly?
If it is a survivor, it learns
to pick the lock."

– ALFA

"She was never crazy.
She just didn't let her heart settle in a cage.
She was born wild. And sometimes we need people like her.
For it's the horrors in her heart which cause the flames in ours.
And she was always willing to burn for everything
she has ever loved."

– R.M. DRAKE

"Somewhere between what she survived
and what she was becoming,
was exactly where she was meant to be.
She was starting to love the journey.
And find the comfort in the quiet corners of her wildest dreams.
They say people don't change….
Well, she wasn't always this way.
Even if she didn't change the entire world,
she would change her part of it.
And she would affect the people she shared it with.
A butterfly whose wings have been touched, can still fly.
Whether something was meant to be, or meant to leave,
didn't matter as much anymore.
She would soak up the sun, kiss the breeze,
and she would fly regardless."

– J. Raymond

"She is the perfect example of grace
because she is a butterfly with bullet holes
in her wings that never regretted
learning to fly."

– JM STORM

3

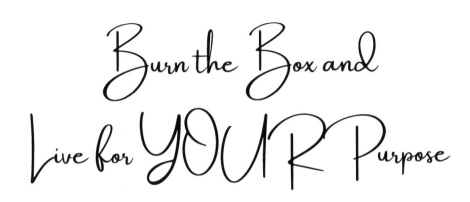

Burn the Box and Live for YOUR Purpose

One of the boxes I was raised in was religion. My parents had different viewpoints on the topic of religion, and for the most part, my father let my mother raise us in the Mormon faith. I often joke that I had a conflicting childhood, but the reality is, I constantly struggled with the religion I was raised in. I have always been one who thinks outside the box and questions everything, and I have always been one who puts a lot of expectations and pressures on myself (many of which are unrealistic). Because I was so hard on myself and the so-called "check-off list" of what makes one worthy in the Mormon faith, I often felt unworthy, all because I couldn't always perfectly meet the requirements or outline of what that religion defined as good and bad, worthy and unworthy. It wasn't because I was ill-behaved or making a lot of poor choices; it was more because I didn't view every item on the check-off list as something that determined one's worth or defined one's character, even though not being able to meet the check-off list caused intense feelings of inadequacy.

When I was twenty, I had a short-lived summer romance, which resulted in getting pregnant with my daughter. I was single, and for the first time in my life, scared to death and had no idea of what I was going to do to provide for and raise a child. Because of how I was raised in the church, I went to the bishop to confess and repent for the sin of having premarital sex. I was excommunicated from the church and told I was no longer worthy of having the Holy Ghost with me. Honestly, I look back and realize that at the age of twenty, I didn't fully understand the concept of the Holy Ghost, but what I do remember vividly, as I sat there feeling scared, alone, and uncertain of the future, was questioning what man or person had the authority and the right to tell me that I was no longer worthy of having what I viewed as the spirit of Christ with me. I felt empty, numb, angry, and completely confused. I was told that being excommunicated was an opportunity for me to be humbled and grow closer to God. And I was "humbled," but their idea of being humbled was more like feelings of embarrassment and shame as I sat in church, trying to "grow closer to God," feeling shunned, judged, and like all eyes were on me.

Many of my family were supportive, while some family and church members urged me to give my daughter up for adoption. They felt she deserved to be born into a family with a mother and a father who was living the gospel and that my opportunities, and hers, would be limited because I was a single parent without a college education. I have always believed there are times where adoption is the right avenue for an individual and is one of the greatest acts of selflessness and love. For me, however, I struggled with the thought of it and could not fathom the idea of not knowing her, loving her, and watching her grow into the woman she would become.

Was that selfish of me? Again, I found myself struggling with this religion's points of view on right and wrong, what defines a family, and so on. How is a child born out of wedlock any less deserving or entitled to being raised and loved by their parent(s)? My beautiful daughter, who was not born under the best of circumstances, saved me and taught me so much about life, who I am, unconditional love, trust, mercy, and hope. In many ways, I look back and realize that she is one of the reasons I am the woman and person that I am today. She truly has been the one constant in my life and the happiest part of every day. I cannot in my wildest imagination look at any of that with guilt or as sin. The irony is that when I look around at the many families who were considered the type of family she "deserved," I realize she and I have the closest relationship, and we have both come out having had more successful opportunities in our lives despite the difficult path we often had.

It was a powerful thing when I was able to finally let go of the "check off list" and the "box" of that religion. I was finally able to see and accept that I am a good person, that I am worthy of unconditional love, and that I do my best to be servant-hearted, honest, and loving to those around me. That integrity, for me, is doing what is right when no one was looking. It took me years to learn that for me, religion and spirituality were two separate things, and to figure out how the belief system I was raised in played a role in my life, both good and bad, and how I viewed myself or believed in myself separately from that. It started with giving myself permission to question it and to take the time to learn what part, if any, resonated with me or didn't. A huge part of that process was found in different life experiences—sometimes by the choices I made and other times by circumstances out of my control.

"Burning the box" is about the idea that we can, as individuals, question the things we are taught and if who we are as an individual resonates with those teachings. It's allowing ourselves to take the time to find out who we are and what we define as right and wrong, what love, service, family, and success mean—what our idea of beauty and self-worth are composed of and are. It's about throwing out the check-off list of traditional and cultural standards and expectations of religion, sexuality, success, and beauty that are keeping you from discovering and growing into the amazing individual and person that you are. It's about giving yourself permission to define your own values, dreams, desires, expectations, and purpose for your life.

"It is often our own thinking that holds us back. Realize this. There's no reason to imprison yourself today. Don't think outside the box. Think like there is no box. Break loose and make the best of the life that is waiting for you."

– Marcandangel

"You are not responsible for the programming you received in your childhood. As an adult, you are 100% responsible for fixing it."

– Unknown

"We do not need to drop everything or break all obligations to pursue our true dreams. But we need not fear dropping or breaking a few things, either."

– BRENDON BURCHARD

"'Finding yourself' is not really how it works. You are not a ten-dollar bill in last winter's coat pocket. You are also not lost. Your true self is right there, buried under cultural conditioning, other people's opinions, and inaccurate conclusions you drew as a kid that became your beliefs about who you are. 'Finding yourself' is actually returning to yourself—an unlearning, an excavation, a remembering of who you were before the world got its hands on you."

– Emily McDowell

"Who you are is perfect.
Our power lies not in becoming someone else
but in unfolding, revealing to the world who we have been created to be.
You don't need to be something else, something different;
who you are is perfect.
So give yourself permission to unfold,
stripping down to the rawest and most authentic version of yourself
and seeing it as brilliant and valuable.
As you do, you'll begin to see yourself living freely
and glowing with light allowing you to experience
the greatness you were destined for."

– LINDSEY ERYN

"It often takes a level of self-love, dedication,
and determination to live your greatest life.
So look within. Look at every area of your life and ask yourself,
'Am I on course? Am I growing mentally, emotionally, and spiritually?'
Anything that is blocking that,
anything that is preventing you from living your greatest life,
make the decision to let it go."

– Unknown

"Sometimes you must step away from limited thinking
and allow life to guide you to plans that are
more significant than you can imagine.
Do not let the fear of you failing keep you stuck
in the comfort zones that block your full potential.
Instead, focus on creating more.
Trust everything is always working out for you.
You are worthy of having at all."

– UNKNOWN

"It's okay to not fit in.
You don't need to bend and break yourself
to simply earn someone's acceptance.
You don't need to spend all your time doing something
you don't even like to earn others' approval.
Learn to be uniquely yourself instead.
Remember that the only ones who ever changed history
were the ones who dared to listen and act upon their own ideas.
They might have been judged and criticized,
but they dared to listen to their own hearts
and changed the world because of it.
So be independent. Be bold…
Because when it really comes down to it,
the only person's acceptance you need
is your own."

– Nikki Banas

"You are free to be who you were created to be.
While the world will do its best to define you,
telling you who to be, how to act, and what to think,
remember: Every fiber of your being was designed with purpose.
The way you think, communicate ideas, and express yourself
is a unique and electric combination that no one else has.
Too often, we misconstrue the evolution of life.
We buy into the idea that we must become someone to be great.
The greatness is already in us.
It's at the core of who we are.
The challenge is to not strive to become something else
but to instead uncover the greatness already within us
by stripping off labels and removing the pressure to blend in
so that we show up in the world as the purest version of ourselves,
completely untainted."

– LINDSEY ERYN

"Do not allow your life to be just fine.
Or okay. Or even good.
Make it brilliant, spectacular, wild, extraordinary.
Fill it with excitement and adventure,
be passionate and fearless,
search for freedom and opportunity.
You only get one life, so make it count.
Make it mean something.
Make it yours."

– Unknown

"Live a life that completely belongs to you.
A life that embraces who you are
and honors your dreams and desires.
A life that lifts you up and supports your healing.
Live a life that is curated by you
and not some societal expectations."

– Unknown

"Do not fear ridicule or rejection.
Fear the consequence of an unlived life
that comes from not expressing yourself
or pursuing your own path."

– BRENDON BURCHARD

"Women are powerful, and I see them stifle this every. Single. Day.
Stop looking to be saved and hiding your magic.
Stop tossing aside your voice and valid emotions.
Stop wasting your time with fake friends
and chasing men like they're cures.
Material things, better jobs, and other people,
they won't fill your gap. Only you can do that.
Life is short.
Rise up and step back into your awesome, innate power.
You are compassion and creative force and divine life itself.
You are a goddess."

– Victoria Erickson

"You must decide if you
are going to rob the
world or bless it with
the rich, valuable,
potent, untapped
resources locked away
within you."

– Myles Munroe

"Fearlessly show up.

Because when you fearlessly show up to do what you were called to do in this world, unconcerned with public opinion, you show up as the most powerful version of yourself, and without a doubt, what you create will pierce through the atmosphere and serve people well.

When you show up, not held back or disabled by people's opinions, you'll move with wisdom and understanding, you'll be bold in your speech and unashamedly speak truth, you'll create with conviction and lead with love, and you'll produce something that radically impacts people's lives, infiltrating their daily life and giving them what they need, not just what they thought they needed or wanted.

So, hold tight to the convictions in your heart, allow truth to lead and guide you as you work and create, and never water down who you are or what you are doing in order to fit in with people or their opinions. You were born to be a leader, not a figurine pushed over or manipulated by opinions."

– Lindsey Eryn

"Sometimes the people with the greatest potential
often take the longest to find their path because
their sensitivity is a double-edged sword – it
lives at the heart of their brilliance,
but it also makes them more susceptible to life's pains.
Good thing we are not penalized for handing in our purpose late.
The soul doesn't know a thing about deadlines."

– JEFF BROWN

"She silently stepped out of the race that she never wanted to be in, found her own lane, and proceeded to win."

– Unknown

Mirror, Mirror on the Wall, Who's the Fairest of Them All?

My mother says that when I was a little girl, I was afraid of mirrors. Because of this, she would put mirrors down along the wall where I was playing so I could get comfortable with them. As I got older, she joked with me that maybe she shouldn't have gotten me so comfortable with them. The truth is, do we as women ever get comfortable with mirrors and what we see when we look in them? And why is that so hard for us? Do we ever get to where we love what we see, where we find beauty in all that makes up the woman looking back at us without noticing or focusing on all the little things we think keep us from feeling or being beautiful?

Beauty. Such a simple word, but a word that we have allowed to have so much power in controlling our belief in ourselves and our self-worth. We have let society define for us what beauty is and what we should see in the mirror to be beautiful. We have accepted this unrealistic idea of what beautiful is, and we spend our whole lives striving to achieve it, all while missing out on understanding and seeing that our beauty, and all the little things that make us beautiful, have always been right in front of us, staring back at us every time we look in the mirror. It isn't found in size, race, physical features, levels of success, or affluence. It's found in our hearts, souls, personalities, love for self and others, the way we laugh, smile, flutter our eyelashes, and cry when we are moved. It's honoring our truth, caring for ourselves, and making healthy choices. It's intelligence, quick wit, and a sense of humor. It's being afraid of the dark and not being afraid to try new things. It's never giving up and giving of ourselves to serve those around us. It's the dimples on our cheeks and the way we squeal when we get excited and scream when we are surprised. The way we carry ourselves with confidence and lift others up. Beauty is all the little things that make us unique and different. There is no single definition of what beauty is or should be because beauty is all the little things that make us who we are. Who you are. And there is only one you.

"Stop apologizing.

You do not have to say sorry for how you laugh, how you dress, how you make your hair, how you do your makeup, how you speak.

You do not have to be sorry for being yourself. Do it fearlessly. It's time to accept this is you, and you got to spend the rest of your life with you.

So start loving your sarcasm, your awkwardness, your weirdness, your peculiar habits, your voice, your talents, your everything. It will make your life so much easier to simply be yourself."

– Cwote

"Do not be beautiful.
They keep saying that beautiful is something a girl needs to be,
but honestly? Forget that. Do not be beautiful.
Be angry, be intelligent, be witty, be klutzy,
be interesting, be funny, be adventurous, be crazy, be talented.
There is an eternity of other things to be other than beautiful.
And what is beautiful anyway but a set of letters strung together to make a word?
Be your own definition of amazing, always.
There is so much more important than anything beautiful, ever."

– Nikita Gill

"Girls don't just simply decide to hate their bodies, we teach them to."

– Unknown

"You have created this mental habit of looking in the mirror
and focusing on things you don't like about yourself.
Parts you feel need to be changed.
How about looking in the mirror
and telling yourself how proud you are of what you have become?
How about looking into your own eyes and feeling the fluidity
and true expression of self-love?
Let it radiate within you. Make this the habit.
The most important person in the world who must love you is you."

– SOURCE MESSAGES

"Sweet girl,
why do you think these thoughts?
You are everything courageous and brave,
intelligent, and witty.
There is a fire in your soul,
burning so bright that stars are jealous.
You will find your way, I promise, and one day,
you will find yourself.
Please do not think these thoughts.
Harsh words do not belong in such
a beautiful mind."

– C.M.T.

"You will never speak to anyone
more than you speak to yourself in your head.
Be kind to yourself.
Be your own supporter."

– UNKNOWN

"Butterflies cannot see their wings.
But the rest of the world can.
You, you are beautiful, and while you may not see it,
we can."

– UNKNOWN

"You don't see yourself the way other people do,
but I wish you could.
The view is breathtaking,
with your heart in your eyes
and the way you carry the whole world on your shoulders
like it has never been heavy."

– Stephanie Bennett-Henry

Not

by Erin Hanson

You are not your age, nor the size of clothes you wear,
You are not a weight or the color of your hair.
You are not your name or the dimples in your cheeks.
You are all the books you read and all the words you speak.
You are your croaky morning voice and the smiles you try to hide.
You're the sweetness in your laughter and every tear you've cried.
You're the songs you sing so loudly when you know you're all alone.
You're the places that you've been to and the one that you call home.
You're the things that you believe in and the people whom you love.
You're the photos in your bedroom and the future you dream of.
You're made of so much beauty, but it seems that you forgot
When you decided that you were defined by all the things you're not.

"You see your reflection in the mirror? Don't be hard on it. Those eyes might look tired, but they have pushed through, carried on. Those lines are of years lived and problems solved. That reflection is one of a brave soul. A warrior, a champion in this world, a healer, a giver, a lover, a sweet spirit. Instead of seeing the flaws, celebrate the good. You are strong, wonderful and more than enough."

– RACHEL MARIE MARTIN

"You have more to do than be weighed down
by pretty or beautiful.
You are a fiery heart and a wicked brain.
Do not let your soul be defined
by its shell."

– UNKNOWN

"Oh honey,
don't worry about being merely beautiful.
Be bold. Be wild. Be strong.
Be confident.
Be independent and intelligent.
Be fierce.
Be brave enough to be real
in this fake world.
Redefine beauty."

– Brooke Hampton

"One day, you will realize how much beauty you have inside you.
How much capacity and light and strength,
and one day, you will realize
how many people you could make a difference in the lives of
if you stopped comparing your life with someone else's
and truly embraced yourself
and activated all you were
meant to be."

– UNKNOWN

"You know what is powerfully sexy?
A sense of humor.
A taste for adventure, a healthy glow, hips to grab on to.
Openness. Confidence. Humility. Appetite.
Intuition. Smart-ass comebacks.
Presence. A quick wit.
Dirty jokes told by an innocent-looking lady.
A woman who realizes how beautiful she is."

– Courtney E. Martin

"Stand in front of the mirror,
look at yourself straight in the eye, and say out loud,
"I love you, I value you,
and I know there is much more to you than what I see staring back at me."
Then close your eyes and repeat the same thing."

– Dr. Wayne Dyer

"And I said to my body, softly,
'I want to be your friend.'
It took a long breath and replied,
'I have been waiting my whole life for this.'"

– NAYYIRAH WAHEED

"You are a beautifully woven
and intricately designed masterpiece, my beautiful friend.
There is not a single soul like yours.
There is not a single person who sees the world how you do.
There is no one who has gone through what you have gone through.
All the ups you've celebrated
and all the downs you've climbed out of.
There is no one who thinks about life the way you do,
nor anyone who interacts with others how you do.
Your identity is entirely your own, my beautiful friend.
You are made of beautiful stories
and life-changing experiences,
you are made of your favorite songs
and the books that have changed you.
You are made of the people you love
and the places you have explored…
Who you are is truly unique and wonderful.
Who you are is worth celebrating
every single day."

– Unknown

"And perhaps what made her beautiful
was not her appearance or what she achieved
but in her love and in her courage and her audacity to believe,
no matter the darkness around her.
Light ran wild within her, and that was the way she came alive,
and it showed up in everything."

– Morgan Harper Nichols

"Be the woman that you are meant to be,
not the woman you think you should be,
or the woman others want you to be.
Look in the mirror and say hello to the warrior Goddess
staring back at you.
Befriend her. Support her. Love her.
And let her open her wings to soar."

– Unknown

5

Flaws Are the New Fabulous

I got picked on a lot as a kid. I was scrawny, a late bloomer, and in many ways, homely. I was made fun of for things going on in my home life. I often felt embarrassment and shame for the chaos that was going on around me, so I taught myself from a very young age to always try and present myself perfectly—the way I dressed, the way I looked, the way I talked, and the way I carried myself were all so people would hopefully think that I was "normal" and had it all together. Without realizing it, I began to set some incredibly high standards for myself regarding what it meant to be "perfect." I spent years working on the "art of perfection." When people commented on how I always looked so perfect and always had it all together, I took such pride.

I received a letter of recommendation from a medical director that I worked for years ago that stated, "Catherine's level of expectations for herself, as well as others, render her incapable of accepting anything less than perfection." He mentioned to me that he wasn't sure if that was a good thing in general, but for the job and responsibilities I had at work, it was.

It took me years to understand what he meant when he stated that he "wasn't sure if that was a good thing." In many areas of my life, those levels of expectations have served me well, and in other areas, they created a misguided perception that for me to be loved or accepted or seen as having value, I had to be perfect.

I felt that people were going to think less of me if they knew some of the struggles I went through, choices I made, or things I tried that did not quite turn out as planned. The irony is, I didn't hold others to those same expectations. I recognized that we all go through struggles. We all make bad choices at times. We all have days that we are not going to look or feel our best. We all have quirks that make us unique and give us character. We all have parts of our personalities that are loving and kind and other parts that are not so loving and kind. I have always wanted people to feel safe "being real" around me, to know that I love and accept them for all those things that make them so unique and wonderful. So why couldn't I accept that others wanted and felt the same thing about me?

I am learning to accept that life is not about always being on stage, being perfect, and always having it all together. Life is messy. It is growing, learning, overcoming, becoming better. We all have strengths, and we all have weaknesses. We all experience success, and we all go through times of struggle. Along with that, I am realizing that I will always have high expectations of myself and strive for excellence; it's how I am wired and who I am, and I am discovering that perfection is not required or what defines excellence. Excellence is about doing your best, and your best may vary at any given time due to circumstances.

"Perfectionism:
a 20-ton shield we lug around
hoping it protects us from experiencing judgment,
shame, and blame,
when all it really does is keep us from being seen.
And it's heavy as f*ck."

– Unlocking Us

"Perfectionism is a self-destructive and addictive belief system
that fills this primary thought:
If I look perfect and do everything perfectly,
I can avoid or minimize the painful feelings of
shame, judgment, and blame."

– BRENE BROWN

"Whatever you are going through right now
is a lesson on accepting yourself.
All of yourself. Even your mistakes. Even your wounds.
Even the things you are in the process of changing.
There is nothing wrong with you,
and there never was."

– Bunny Michael

"You strive so hard to please them all,
thinking you can somehow prove your worth,
and your validity. Imagine if you wanted the same approval
from your own self."

– ALFA

"Perfection does not protect you from being hurt, but from being seen."

– UNKNOWN

"When perfectionism is driving, shame is always riding shotgun."

– Brene Brown

"Perfection is annihilation.
It paralyzes us from working from the heart.
Humans by nature are not perfect,
and imperfections are what make the world beautiful."

– Unknown

"Some days you will give the
world and some days you'll
feel you can't give a thing.
Some days you will move
mountains and some days you'll
feel you can't move yourself
out of bed. Some days you will
tell stories late into the night
and some days you won't find
one word to accurately express
what it is you are feeling.
I just want you to know you
are beautiful. You are worthy
of love and your presence is
still needed in this world
on both kinds of days."

– S.C. Lourie

"What we don't need in the midst of struggle is shame for being human."

– Brene Brown

"To work on yourself is the best thing you can do.
Accept that you are not perfect, but you are enough.
And then start working on everything that destroys you.
Your insecurities, your ego, your dark thoughts.
You will see, in the end, you're going to make peace with yourself,
and that's the greatest thing in the world."

– UNKNOWN

"At the end of the day, I'm a good woman.
I'm not perfect by any means, but my intentions are good,
my heart is pure, and I love hard with everything I've got,
and because of those things, I'm worth it.
Always have been and always will be."

– UNKNOWN

"Self-love
Be brave enough to take off the masks
you wear out there and get to know who
you are underneath. Be vulnerable
enough to accept your flaws and know
that they are what make you human; they
are what make you real. Be confident
enough to accept and cherish your
strengths. Don't minimize or hide
them. They are your beautiful gifts to
the world. Be brave enough to
say, you know what, all of this is who I
am. I make so many mistakes. I can be
forgetful, I am messy. But…I am doing
my best with what I've got. And I am so
proud of that. I am so proud of me. And I
am proud of who I am becoming."

– Nikki Banas

"Perfectionism is really fear wearing a costume."

– Allegra Sinclair

"I dare you to take off the mask of perfection and show up as you are,
feel the freedom, the relief, the lightness.
Because when we are real, that's when we actually heal.
And those around us just may heal too."

– Ashley Hetherington

"I hope you remember that when you let people see the messy,
flawed, goofy reality of you,
it's like you're giving them a gift.
Some people won't appreciate it, but others will smile with relief
and recognition and say,
'Oh, thank goodness I'm not the only one.'"

– NANNIES HOFFMAN

"I think midlife is when the universe gently places her hands upon your shoulders,
pulls you close and whispers in your ear:
I'm not screwing around. It's time. All this pretending and performing,
these coping mechanisms that you've developed to protect yourself
from feeling inadequate and getting hurt, has to go.
Your armor is preventing you from growing into your gifts.
I understand that you needed these protections when you were small.
I understand that you believed your armor could help you secure all the things you
needed to feel worthy of love and belonging,
but you're still searching, and you're more lost than ever.
Time is growing short. There are unexplored adventures ahead of you.
You can't live the rest of your life worried about what other people think.
You were born worthy of love and belonging.
Courage and daring are coursing through you.
You were made to live and love with your whole heart.
It's time to show up and be seen."

– BRENE BROWN

"Look at yourself and see how beautiful and luminous you are. Let go of your yearning for perfection. Everything is as it should be—complete."

– Wholistic, Inc.

"And then there are women like me:
no longer afraid to show people that we're human,
and that we cry, hurt, scream, and feel weak sometimes, just like everyone else.
We stopped apologizing for not being perfect a long time ago
because we've learned that perfect isn't even a real thing.
We've learned that strength isn't about being bulletproof, but instead,
about the will to survive the bullets
and being able to forgive those who have fired them at us,
not for their peace of mind… but for our own.
Women like me don't pretend anymore to have it all together 24/7.
We're growing through life one day at a time and doing the best we can.
One day at a time."

– CICI B.

"There are parts of me that will remain untamable, messy, and reckless. But I refuse to apologize for it anymore."

– KAITLIN FOSTER

6

Beautifully Broken

There comes a time, whether you are ready for it or not, that the impact, hurt, and effects of former traumas, abuse, loss, and betrayals you have experienced will surface and stare you straight in the face. Regardless of how well you learned that "if you don't talk about it, it never happened and doesn't exist." The first time I recall learning that approach and mindset was when I was a young child and had been sexually molested. How was I to know at such a young age that along with accepting and adopting that mindset, I would also be bringing along all the things that went with it—things like shame, embarrassment, blaming myself, anger, resentment, trust issues, and unhealthy coping mechanisms? And how was I to know that all of that would set the stage for how I reacted, faced, and dealt with other traumatic events and difficult times later in my life? One of those coping mechanisms I learned early on was to just "be strong." And I was. And I am. I have a lot of strength and resiliency that are just innately part of my character and who I am. There came a time, however, that I had to learn and accept that strength does not mean keeping it all bottled in, tucked away, and buried. Denial and pretending that painful and difficult events did not have an impact or play a role in certain areas of my life doesn't work.

True strength is allowing yourself to go through whatever it takes to heal. And for someone like me who likes to have everything neat and tidy and in its place, realizing that there is no guidebook, time frame, or one-size-fits-all approach to healing from trauma, loss, grief, and suffering regardless of what it is that has broken your heart and spirit. It is acknowledging it, talking about it, giving yourself permission to be angry, vulnerable, and taking time to feel and work through the pain. To recognize how it has changed and made me who I am, how I view life, and how I move forward in life. But most of all that I can feel and be completely broken at times and still be beautiful, strong, and worthy of being loved.

"There are moments that will mark your life,
moments when you realize nothing will ever be the same
and time is divided into two parts:
before this and after this."

– Unknown

"Trauma is perhaps the most avoided,
ignored, belittled, denied,
misunderstood, and untreated cause
of human suffering."

– Peter Levine

"What you deny or ignore,
you delay. What you accept and face,
you conquer."

– Robert Tew

"Forgive yourself for survival patterns you picked up while enduring trauma."

– Unknown

"Maybe you were holding it together for someone else's sake,
and I'm proud of you for being strong,
but sometimes we have to break to find healing in the pieces.
It's okay to let go and save yourself."

– Stephanie Bennett-Henry

"No one is going to help you get better.
No one is going to heal you, to make you get over it and move on.
Sometimes you have to repair what's broken on your own.
And sometimes you have to face what hurts you by yourself."

– R.M. Drake

"There will be very painful moments in your life that will change you.
Let them make you stronger, smarter, and kinder.
But don't you go and become someone you are not. Cry. Scream if you must.
Then straighten out that crown and keep moving."

– Unknown

"Don't hide your hurt, beautiful soul.
Grab hold of it. Run it through the purifying flame of your heart
and mold it into something beautiful.
Allow the depths of your pain to expand the breadth of your compassion.
Gather up your stumbling stones and build a bridge for someone else
to remember what it's like to be lost in darkness
so you can be someone else's much-needed light.
Don't deny your pain or bury it away. Let it rise to the surface.
And then transform it into something that makes it worthwhile."

– CRISTEN RODGERS

"When you survive loss, everyone is quick to tell you how strong you are
and how tough you must be.
But actually, no one has a choice to survive grief.
It's not optional. You just have to cry in the shower, sob in your pillow,
and pray you will make it."

– Zoe Clark-Coates

"Allow yourself to go through the aftermath but at your own pace.
To grieve. To cry. To feel. Trust yourself when it hurts.
Allow yourself to hurt. It's okay.
You have to understand that these moments of pain are
just as important as the good times.
These are the moments that will define you. The moments that will test you.
Break you. And place you back together again."

– R.M. Drake

"We must not give up.
It takes so much time to heal because
we are not just healing our own wounds-
we are healing the world's wounds too.
We think we are alone with our "stuff", but we aren't.
With every clearing of our emotional debris,
with every foray into a healthier way of being,
with every excavation and release of old material,
we heal the collective heart.
So many of our familial and karmic ancestors
had little opportunity to heal their pains.
When we heal, their spirits breathe a sigh of relief.
We heal them backwards, while healing ourselves forward.
We heal in unison."

– Jeff Brown

"There is a sacredness in tears.
They are not the mark of weakness but of power.
They speak more eloquently than 10,000 tongues.
They are the messengers of overwhelming grief,
of deep contrition, and unspeakable love."

– Washington Irving

"Sit with your emotions as they arise.
Feel them, listen to them, appreciate them, but never run from them,
because they'll track you down and haunt you until
you are courageous enough to face them
and ultimately learn the lessons that they hold."

– UNKNOWN

"It's ok if you thought you were over it,
but it hits you all over again.
It's okay to fall apart even after you thought you had it under control.
You are not weak. Healing is messy. There is no timeline for healing."

– Unknown

"Your anger is the part of you that knows your mistreatment
and abuse are unacceptable.
Your anger knows you deserve to be treated well and with kindness.
Your anger is a part of you that loves you."

– Unknown

"Honestly, with time, you'll come to understand
that the frantic, extremely anxious,
broken, and unhinged version of you
was absolutely nothing to be ashamed of.
You know why?
Because you were simply a kindhearted person
who was reacting to a very unkind situation.
And the thing is that no one will tell you this.
No one will tell you this because no one knows the intensity of the pain
that crawled out of the shattering noises of your broken world.
What happened to you was really unkind,
and how you felt was not your fault."

– EXCERPTS OF HER STORY

"Life isn't always filled with sunshine and beauty,
but I believe you can learn so much more from the darker and uglier side of living.
If only you are willing to go and grow through it.
It's okay to not be perfect in this imperfect world, and it's okay to have doubts and fears.
It's okay to be messy and disturbed, and it's damn sure okay to feel broken.
But I'll say this: It's not okay to put yourself in a prison
when you were merely supposed to be planted.
So get in the dirt and feel every ounce of pain and discomfort,
but when you finally find your roots once more
and the light begins to touch your skin,
you must break that ground with confidence and rise.
You have always been destined to do just that."

– M.F.

"Healing does not mean the damage never existed.
It means the damage no longer controls our lives."

– Unknown

"To recover is to create a life in which numbness
is no longer necessary for survival."

– UNKNOWN

"When recovering from a difficult thing such as
heart break or traumatic experience,
stop trying to find your old self.
The old you doesn't exist anymore.
Look for the new and improved version of you."

– UNKNOWN

"No one will ever fully be able to understand
the internal battles you had to endure just to heal,
just to grow, just to make it here today.
Be proud of the way you saved yourself.
Be proud of the way you survived."

– Unknown

"Vulnerability is not weakness.
It's our most accurate measure of courage."

– BRENE BROWN

"In the end, it was her brokenness that became her superpower.
The moment she realized that her vulnerability was also her strength,
she saved herself instead."

– James McInerney

"She was walking proof
that you can have your soul torn in half
and still navigate through life
beautifully."

– Alfa

"Healing makes you realize how beautiful,
divine, whole, and worthy
you always were."

– Unknown

7
Own Your Story

Another "exercise" I was given in the pursuit of getting back to "me" was to write out my life story from the earliest memory I had to the present moment. This was harder for me than I expected. There were moments I was proud of and was excited to write about. And then there were moments, memories, and times in my life that I had spent years keeping safely tucked away, buried in the cobwebs of my soul—childhood traumas, failed relationships, being a young single parent with no college education, the list seemed to go on and on.

"Why in the hell was she having me do this exercise?!" I not only struggled to write it, but I struggled even more to go back and read it. I couldn't read it without sobbing and feeling shame, guilt, embarrassment, and failure.

And then the unthinkable happened. I was challenged to find someone that I trusted to share it with. Did she not realize what she was asking me to do, what she was asking of this person who was still struggling to "let people in," and accepting that I don't have to be perfect to be worthy of people's love and acceptance? I soon learned that she knew exactly what she was doing.

It took me a while, but I finally thought of someone I trusted, someone who believed in me and held me in high regard, and someone who I felt respected me and was proud of the various accomplishments I had achieved in my life. They agreed to let me share it with them. The moment I hit send on the email, an incredible panic set in, and I started sobbing. All I could think about was what they would think of me once they read everything. Would they still respect me? Would they still hold me in such high regard? Would they still like me as a person and be proud of me? The wait for their response was agonizing and felt like an eternity. And then I got their reply.

It was nothing I had expected. Their response was filled with so much love and kindness. They said that I was looking at my story all wrong. Instead of feeling like a failure, full of shame and embarrassment, I should feel proud of myself for choosing to not let any of those things hold me back—to be proud of all the times things did not work out and I had the courage to pick up the pieces and start over. For all the moments that caused me so much pain, yet I still had a heart full of love, kindness, and compassion for others. That I had raised a daughter who had grown into a beautiful, strong, kind, successful woman and loving parent. They shared how impressed they were with everything I had accomplished despite all that I had been through and how I should acknowledge how all those moments, heartaches, challenges, and triumphs throughout my life helped make me the incredible woman they knew today. That I needed to take all the shame, embarrassment, and guilt and "put it in a box, wrap it up and place a pretty little bow on it, and take it out to the curb for the trash to pick up." I sat there speechless (and sobbing) for quite a while. I read their response over and over. This was one of the kindest gifts anyone had ever given me, and I needed to give myself this gift of love and kindness as well.

It isn't easy and takes time to shift your thought process from feeling shame for the parts of your story that aren't so easy to write and read, to feeling pride for having had the strength to overcome weakness, obstacles, or trials you have faced—to acknowledge that you had the strength to get through it and are still standing.

Start telling yourself what you love about yourself, recognize your talents and strengths, and celebrate what you have accomplished and are working toward rather than criticizing yourself for the times in your life that that didn't go as planned, that caused you incredible pain and sorrow, that forced you to stretch and grow. Your story, up until this point, is what makes you the incredible woman that you are. And your story is not over. Your story going forward is still yet to be written, and the beautiful thing is, you hold the pen. Take it and write and design what the rest of your story will look like going forward, the story that honors and supports the incredible woman you are and the one you are still becoming.

"We all have a bag. We all pack it differently.
Some of us are traveling light.
Some of us are secret hoarders who have never parted with a memory in our lives.
I think we are all called to figure out how to carry our bag to the best of our ability,
how to unpack it, and how to face the mess.
I think part of growing up is learning how to sit on the floor with all your things
and figuring out what to take with you
and what to leave behind."

– Hannah Brencher

"It takes years as a woman
to unlearn what you have been taught
to be sorry about."

– AMY POEHLER

"You should dance with the skeletons in your closet.
Learn their names, so you can ask them to leave.
Have coffee with your demons.
Ask them important questions like, 'What keeps you here?'
Learn what doors they keep finding open and
kick them out."

– MICHELLE MCGRAW

"You either walk inside your story and own it,
or you stand outside your story
and hustle for your worthiness."

– Brene Brown

"Release the shame and guilt from your past
and accept how things have transpired.
Your past shortcomings taught you valuable lessons
that can help you become a better person.
Use your pain to create your greatest victory."

– ASH ALVES

"Never be embarrassed by your struggle.
Never apologize for the things you've worked hard for.
Every part of your journey has beauty in it,
so never let anyone drag you down for climbing
to a better place."

– Vex King

"You've been through a thousand things in your life
people don't even know about.
You've experienced things that have shaken you.
Changed you, broke you, built you, and taught you to be stronger
than you ever thought you had the ability to be.
And you are who you are for all of it.
So the next time someone judges you based on a small part
of what they see and how they interpret that,
remember who you are, remember how much you have overcome,
and smile and keep walking
because you don't have a single thing to prove to anyone else.
You've already proven so much to yourself,
who muddled through storms that people didn't even see
because of how you carried yourself."

– KIRSTEN CORLEY

"Life's like that.
You'll carry the burdens, emotional or otherwise,
day in and day out for so long and never realize their effects.
Time to let go,
because sometimes you won't feel the weight of something
you're carrying until you feel the weight
of its release."

– S. L.

"I am still learning how to go back
and re-read my own chapters
without feeling like I want to set
all my pages on fire."

– E.V. Regina

"It's easy to look back and question decisions you have made in the past,
but it's unfair to punish yourself for them.
You can't blame yourself for not knowing back then what you know now,
and the truth is you made each decision for a reason,
based on how you were feeling at the time.
As we grow up, we learn, and we evolve.
Maybe the person you are now would have done things differently back then.
Or maybe you are the person you are now
because of the decisions you made back then.
Trust your journey; it's all going to make sense soon."

– Unknown

"The irony is we attempt to disown our difficult stories
to appear more whole and more acceptable,
but our wholeness, even our whole-heartedness, actually
depends on the integration of all our experiences,
including the falls."

– Brene Brown

"Your story isn't calm.

The road has been chaotic at times,

filled with detours and rain and loss so sudden and soon.

Sometimes the bliss was so elevated your heart could hardly hold it.

Sometimes it was maddening to have and then to lose.

You learn soon enough that it hardly ever goes as planned.

Gentle, easy, and smooth.

But that, my friend, is what makes you fascinating.

You have something to tell. Something you've walked through.

Something wild. Something courageous. Something true.

You're made of stories within stories within even more stories.

Those quiet depths of you."

– Victoria Erickson

"There is freedom and there is magic
in being honest about who you are
and what you've been through."

– Unknown

"The butterfly does not look back at the caterpillar in shame,
just as you should not look back at your past in shame.
Your past was part of your own transformation."

– Anthony Gucciardi

"Learn from what's behind you,
but look forward to what's ahead.
It would be a sad, sad existence if you believed
your best has already come and gone.
Believe instead the truth,
that the best is yet to be,
because that part is up to you."

– UNKNOWN

"Instead of focusing on all the things you missed out on
and all the times and ways that you held yourself back,
limited, betrayed, or sabotaged yourself,
start counting all the ways that you're going to encourage yourself
to do your best and to be your best self.
It's time to release the guilt, shame, and resentment
that you've been holding onto regarding your past.
It's subtly spoiling your future.
Start saying 'yes' to life and promise yourself
that you're not going to hide away from life anymore.
Ultimately, there is still so much more in store for you."

– MESSAGE OF LOVE

"We are not defined by the events in our lives,
but rather by the narrative we write for ourselves
in response to those events."

– Dave Manning

"Our job is not to deny the story
but to defy the ending. To rise strong, recognize our story,
and rumble with the truth
until we get to a place where we think,
'Yes, this is what happened.
This is my truth.
And I will choose how the story ends.'"

– Brene Brown

"You are rare—a hidden beauty waiting to be discovered.
You are the best kind of beautiful—a mosaic of scars and radiance.
A delicate combination of facets, unveiling everything you have been through.
Parts of you have seen the dark, have endured the pain of loss,
and have encountered the disappointment of betrayal.
Please do not hide these fragments of who you are
in fear of feeling incomplete or unworthy of love.
Everything you have been through has allowed you to grow
and flourish into the best version of yourself.
Please remember that not all diamonds are cut the same—
you can be flawed yet still cascade light. You can be fractured yet still be complete.
You are a diamond in the rough—imperfect yet invaluable.
Do not doubt the brilliance of your own light.
If you work to love all your facets,
you'll shine brighter than everything around you."

– BRYAN ANTHONYS

"The most beautiful people we have known
are those who have known defeat, known suffering,
known struggle, known loss, and have found their way out of the depths.
These persons have an appreciation, a sensitivity,
and an understanding of life that fills them with compassion,
gentleness, and a deep loving concern.
Beautiful people do not just happen."

– Elizabeth Kubler-Ross

"She wore her troubled past like scars.
She had been through battle, and though no one could see her
demons, they could see the face that conquered them."

– ATTICUS

"She's been through more hell than you'll ever know.
But that's what gives her beauty an edge…
You can't touch a woman who can wear pain
like the grandest of diamonds
around her neck."

– ALFA

"Sometimes God redeems your story
by surrounding you with people who need to hear your past,
so it doesn't become their future."

– JOHN ACUFF

"Share your story; you never know who it will inspire.
Speak your truth even if your voice shakes.
There are times when your voice will not be as strong,
allow others to help you find it again.
Don't die with your song still inside you."

– UNKNOWN

"Let the story of who you were
send shivers down the spines of our granddaughters.
Let them hear about you as the woman who was 'herself,'
who did her own thing and helped others along the way."

– Tanya Markul

"My story is filled with broken pieces,
terrible choices, and very ugly truths,
but it's also filled with a major comeback,
peace in my soul, and a grace that saved my life."

– UNKNOWN

"Look back at where you came from
and let yourself feel proud about your progress.
You. Are. Killing it."

– Unknown

8

Failure Is Not the Other F-Word

Failure has always been an interesting word for me. I have always looked at it two different ways, depending on the circumstance. If it was a mistake or a bad decision that I considered a failure, then I would be incredibly hard on myself and let it impact my feelings of self-worth and belief in myself in a negative way. Failure, then, is another F-word that I do not say or talk about. And if I do talk about it, I often feel like I need to justify and apologize for it.

On the flip side, if I am trying something new, taking on a challenge headfirst, or proving that something can be done, especially when someone said it was impossible, then failure was just part of the process and was the fuel that fed my determination to succeed. It has a positive impact on my self-worth and belief in myself, and it is okay to talk about it. The difference is when I speak about that type of failure, it is in a positive light, and it becomes what helps me ultimately accomplish whatever it is that I am trying to do.

Why do we sometimes expect and even allow ourselves to fail and to struggle, and in other circumstances, we beat ourselves up and feel as if failing is a shortcoming? Regardless of the circumstance, the mistakes, struggles, and failures mean you are living. You are trying and taking chances.

Be proud of that. Be proud that you are amongst the ones who are not afraid to take risks. Use those opportunities to learn and grow. Know that they have helped shape and define the person that you are and that you are smarter, more knowledgeable, and capable of so much more because of them. Use them as the fuel that continues to feed your determination, desire, and ability to grow and succeed.

"If you look back only at your mistakes,
you will think you were an idiot.
If you look back at only your wiser choices,
you will think you were infallible.
But if you look back on everything,
you realize you are a human being
who has been through a lot,
grown a lot, is always still learning,
and improving as time goes by."

– DOE ZANTAMATA

"You can disappoint people and still be good enough.
You can fail and still be smart, capable, and talented.
You can let people down and still be worthwhile and
deserving of love and admiration.
We all make mistakes sometimes.
Take a deep breath.
You are allowed to be human."

– MARCANDANGEL

"Everyone makes bad choices in their lives,
but that does not mean they have to pay for them the rest of their lives.
Sometimes good people make bad choices.
It does not mean they are bad.
It means they are human."

– Unknown

"Make bold choices and make mistakes.
It's all those things that add up to
the person you become."

– ANGELINA JOLIE

"You are still punishing yourself
for things you did when you did not know any better.
Stop sabotaging your future."

– Unknown

"Forgive yourself.

Forgive yourself for what happened.

For the mistakes you made. For the poor choices.

For not showing up the way you needed to. For not being the person, you wanted to be.

You're human.

You did the best you could in the moment, given what you knew and what you had, and that's all you can ask of yourself. You're still learning. You're still finding your way. And that takes time. You're allowed to give yourself that time. And you're allowed to show up in the world imperfectly. You're allowed to fail at things you tried hard for. You're allowed to realize you made the wrong decision. You're allowed to be someone who is still figuring out their path and their purpose. And you're allowed to forgive yourself. You can't go back and change the decisions you've made, but you can choose what you do today. You can keep choosing, again and again. You can start over. And that's where your power is. In today. So, no more beating yourself up. No more going over and over it again in your head and torturing yourself with the past. What happened, happened, and all the shame and self-hatred in the world won't undo that. Today, you're starting over. Today, you are moving forward with the new knowledge and experiences you have. Today you can be the person you want to be and live the life you want to live.

You're not a bad person.

You're not a disappointment or a failure. You're just human.

And you're still learning and growing and finding your way.

And it's okay. You'll be okay."

– Daniell Koepke

"When you forgive yourself,
you create the space to be a better version of yourself
instead of clinging to the old version of yourself
that you want to punish."

– MICHELLE MAROS

"Do your thing.
Do it every day. Do it unapologetically.
Don't be discouraged by criticism.
Pay no mind to the fear of failure.
It's far more valuable than success.
Take ownership, take chances, and have fun.
And no matter what,
don't ever stop doing your thing."

– Asher Roth

"If you are not in the arena also getting your ass kicked,
I am not interested in your feedback."

– Brene Brown

"Of course, I stumble.
There are times when I'm confidently skipping along
and then I trip over my own poorly placed steps
and fall face-first into the thickets.
But I think there is sort of a beauty in falling.
Each time I fall, I'm reminded that I'm still human,
that I'm still learning, that there will always be more lessons,
growth, and discovery up ahead.
So, although I have times when I am weak,
when I'm critical of myself, or I lose hope,
I wouldn't give them up for the world.
I cherish them because it's the risk of falling
that makes life a grand adventure
rather than just a guided tour."

– CRISTEN RODGERS

"Don't ever be ashamed of your scars.
Scars, although painful, mean that you're still
here and that you got through it.
The reason may not be so clear.
But maybe, just maybe, that reason is
so that you can be a light
to those who are hoping to do
just that….get through it."

– AMANDA FERNANDEZ

"Hard times are often blessings in disguise.
Let go and let life strengthen you.
No matter how much it hurts, hold your head up and keep going.
This is an important lesson to remember when you are having a rough day,
a bad month, or a crappy year.
Truth be told, sometimes the hardest lessons to learn are
the ones your spirit needs the most.
Your past was never a mistake if you learn from it.
So, take all the crazy experiences and lessons
and place them in a box
labeled thank you."

– Unknown

"Bravery is the audacity to be unhindered by failures,
and to walk with freedom,
strength, and hope,
in the face of things unknown."

– Morgan Harper Nichols

"Think like a queen.
A queen is not afraid to fail.
Failure is another steppingstone
to greatness."

– Oprah Winfrey

9

Self-Love Does Not Spell Selfish

Women are incredible, resilient, strong individuals who are often the ones who juggle it all, hold everything together, all while doing whatever it takes to make it happen. We tend to be empathetic and compassionate, focused on nurturing those around us, putting everyone's needs above our own. Yet we often feel guilty for taking time to care for ourselves, for putting our needs and wants first, for throwing up the white flag at times to say, "I need a break." We think it's a sign of weakness to say, "I need to just sit here and take a moment to rest and catch my breath." We feel like we are selfish when we choose ourselves above everyone else, regardless of whether it is our family, friends, or even our co-workers.

When you recognize that people or situations are causing you harm, suffering and are no longer healthy for your wellbeing, give yourself permission to make your needs and wellbeing a priority without feeling guilty for it.

Allow yourself time to breathe, to rest and turn off all the noise and distraction and disconnect from the world around you, to reconnect with your inner spirit. It is not selfish. It is self-love. It is a necessity and one that needs to be a priority—not only for yourself but for those you love and want to be there for. It goes back to that old saying: "You cannot pour from an empty cup." When you are doing well, everyone around you will do so much better. Taking care of yourself is the most unselfish thing you can do and the best gift that you can give, not only to yourself, but to your family and those around you.

"You don't owe anyone for anything.
But you do owe yourself quite a bit.
Start with apologizing for all the times you put yourself last.
It's okay to put yourself first, and it's okay to call yourself beautiful.
You owe it to you. I just wanted you to know."

– STEPHANIE BENNETT-HENRY

"Saying no to people, places, and circumstances
that make you feel bad about yourself
is the highest act of self-care."

– MICHELLE MAROS

"You have to learn to say no without feeling guilty.
Setting boundaries is healthy.
You need to learn to respect and
take care of yourself."

– UNKNOWN

"When I loved myself enough,
I began leaving whatever wasn't healthy.
Unhealthy people, jobs, my own beliefs, and habits,
anything that kept me small.
My judgment called it disloyal.
Now I see it as self-love."

– UNKNOWN

"It is important to do what's best for you,
whether people approve it or not, this is your life.
You know what is good for you, and remember,
self-love takes strength."

– UNKNOWN

"The truth is sometimes we change our minds about love,
and 'I love you' becomes 'I don't know if I can do this anymore.'
Sometimes, 'I'll stay with you forever'
becomes 'I have to leave before I lose my mind.'
And sometimes 'I'll never break your heart' becomes
'I need to take care of my heart now.'"

– Rania Naim

"I will not stay, not ever again,
in a room or conversation or relationship or situation
that requires me to abandon myself."

– Glennon Doyle

"There are bigger goals in life than being a good woman to a man.

Be a good woman to yourself first."

– Karen Civil

"I hate it when people say, 'They are still your family.'
Just because someone is your family does not mean
you must keep them in your life if they are toxic.
Blood means nothing sometimes.
Do not let people guilt you into being in contact
with someone who is not good for your mental health."

– Unknown

"There are some of us women who have put focusing
on ourselves at the top of our to-do list,
and it's not because we're angry or bitter from being fresh off a heartbreak.
But rather because, for some of us, turning our dreams into living realities is important.
Learning how to be comfortable standing on our own two feet is important.
Setting goals and meeting those goals is important.
Creating an identity for ourselves and being who we want to be
in this world without having to check with anyone else
to see if it's OK with them first is important."

– Cici B.

"If your compassion does not include yourself, it is incomplete."

– ALAN WATTS

"Your energy will fluctuate from high to low very easily.
Some days, you feel like conquering the world.
Other days, you feel like cuddling with your pillows.
Both are equally empowering, and both are equally necessary.
You didn't come into this life to exhaust yourself.
Embrace the days that call for self-love, relaxation, and pampering yourself.
You deserve to be physically and mentally carefree."

– Source Messages

"Promise yourself things will change this time,
and you will start taking care of yourself.
Promise yourself you will start eating healthier and taking care of your body.
Promise yourself you will make sure you get enough sleep,
and you will focus on thoughts that build you up
instead of thoughts that tear you down and eat you up inside.
Promise to be gentle and kind to yourself
and to remind yourself that you are doing the best you can,
and although you are still growing and improving,
in this very moment, you are enough.
And promise yourself you will learn to love yourself
enough to keep the promises
you make to yourself."

– Unknown

Self-love

"You must choose yourself, even when others refuse to.
Self-love is choosing yourself and choosing yourself is self-care.
You're entertaining the wrong things with the wrong people
because you're struggling with loving yourself.
It's okay to take a break, a moment for yourself.
It's okay to be selfish if it means re-discovering
your own power and happiness."

– R.H. SIN

"Fall in love with taking care of yourself.
Fall in love with the path of deep healing.
Fall in love with the best version of yourself
but with patience, compassion,
and respect for your own journey."

– Sylvester McNutt III

"Your relationship with yourself sets the tone for every other relationship you have."

– ROBERT HOLDEN

"Once you realize your worth, you'll be embarrassed at the shit you once settled for."

– AMBRY MEHR

"Self-love is the greatest middle finger of all time."

– Unknown

"The most valuable lesson I have ever learned
from the most painful times in my life
is to always choose myself.
Today I choose me."

– Stephanie Bennett-Henry

"I was a good girl who had a bad habit
of putting other people's wants and needs above my own.
I'm still a good girl though…it's just that now I have a good habit
of using the word 'no' whenever I need to,
and not feeling the slightest bit guilty about it."

– CICI B.

"I will not apologize for choosing myself this time.
Self-love is the chapter that I've always wanted to write."

– S. R. W.

"A woman who loves is powerful.
A woman who loves herself
is unstoppable."

– Unknown

10

No U-Turns Ahead

Change is one of those words that can have both positive and negative emotions associated with it. There are times in life that we look forward to the possibility of a change so much that we lose sight of the present moment we are in. Then there are times when the fear of change and uncertainty is so great that we become completely stuck in our present situation…even if it is not the best thing for us.

There are times that we have change thrust upon us, completely out of our control, where we have no choice but to accept and embrace the changes we are facing. There are also times when we will be the only one that can take control, and make the changes necessary for our growth, physical and emotional well-being, a more positive and healthier environment, and the chance for a brighter future. Even when we are the ones choosing to make a change, it can still be hard—hard to step away from all that we know, what has been our comfort zone and what we have learned to expect and control. The uncertainty of what lies ahead can make us want to look back and question whether the change we are considering is necessary. The decision to make a change becomes so overwhelming that we ultimately choose to do nothing. And if we find the courage to make a change, once we start feeling the uncertainty, and sometimes difficulty of what lies ahead, we turn right around and go back to what it is that we were considering changing. The comfort in knowing what to expect outweighs the faith, vulnerability, and discomfort that change often requires.

Sometimes it isn't about a physical change, but rather a change in how you believe or view things, what defines you or makes you happy. All these things can change as you grow as an individual and have different experiences in life. You are allowed to, at any moment, decide that certain beliefs, old ways of thinking, situations, people, or environments are no longer healthy or honor who you are and make changes where you feel necessary.

"Your new life is going to cost you your old one.

It's going to cost you your comfort zone and your sense of direction.

It's going to cost you your relationships and friends.

It's going to cost you being liked and understood.

But it doesn't matter.

Because the people who are meant for you are going to meet you on the other side.

And you're going to build a new comfort zone

around the things that actually move you forward.

And instead of liked, you're going to be loved.

Instead of understood, you're going to be seen.

All you're going to lose is what was built for a person you no longer are.

Let it go."

– Brianna Wiest

"Dozens of times throughout your life, you will outgrow
what you thought you couldn't live without
and fall in love with what you didn't even know you wanted.
Life will lead you on hard yet necessary paths
you would never travel by choice.
Do not be afraid. Have faith.
Trust the journey."

– MARCANDANGEL

SHINE ON, YOU CRAZY DIAMOND

"When it's time for you to step into something greater,
do not stop the process by being afraid of what comes next
or staying the same just because it's comfortable.
It's okay to evolve and outgrow people.
It's also perfectly fine not to know what comes next.
Just go on and don't look back."

– Unknown

Fear

It is said that before entering the sea
a river trembles with fear.

She looks back at the path she has traveled,
from the peaks of the mountains,
the long winding road crossing forests and villages.

And in front of her,
she sees an ocean so vast
that to enter
there seems nothing more than to disappear forever.

But there is no other way.
The river cannot go back.

Nobody can go back.
To go back is impossible in existence.

The river needs to take the risk
of entering the ocean
because only then will fear disappear,
because that's where the river will know
it's not about disappearing into the ocean,
but of becoming the ocean.

– KAHLIL GIBRAN

"Maybe it's not about trying to fix something broken.
Maybe it's about starting over
and creating something better."

– Unknown

"Do not be afraid to start over.
This time you are not starting from scratch,
you are starting from experience."

– UNKNOWN

"It's hard to leave toxic situations because that has been your comfort zone for so long.
But once you cleanse your space,
you will realize that you were drinking poison and calling it medicine.
Spit it out.
You were standing in hell and calling it peace, holding red flags and waving them like a truce.
You went up in flames and said it was not too hot.
And now you are afraid of being too cold without that comfort zone.
Break the ice, love.
There is a whole world waiting on the other side,
where nothing ever burns."

– STEPHANIE BENNETT-HENRY

"Never forget that walking away from something unhealthy is brave,
even if you stumble a little on your way out the door."

– MANDY HALE

"Some of us run back to situations that cause nothing but repeated pain. Our hearts will never heal if we keep making them love backward."

– ALFA

"You have to quit other people to save yourself sometimes.
You have to unbreak long enough to realize they quit you first,
and there is nothing to hold onto.
So pick up the pieces, hold them close,
and become whole once again by yourself."

– Stephanie Bennett-Henry

"Even though there are days I wish I could change
some things that happened in the past,
there's a reason the rear-view mirror is so small,
and the windshield is so big.
Where you are headed is more important
than what you have left behind."

– Unknown

"One day, you will look back at all the stormy days
of your past, and you will accept that the wreckage you sifted through
was never meant to be rebuilt."

– ALFA

"You will know you made the right decision
when you feel the stress leaving your body,
your mind, your life."

– Brigitte Nicole

"Every woman that finally figured out her worth
has picked up her suitcases of pride and boarded a flight to freedom,
which landed in the valley of change."

– SHANNON L. ALDER

"She got tired of saying the same things, fighting the same battles,
and playing the same games.
Shoulders relaxed, crown up, and head held high,
the queen walked away for the very last time."

– Unknown

11

When the Crown Feels Heavy, Celebrate Your Strength

There are times that life is simply hard and will undoubtedly let you down no matter how hard you are trying and no matter how much focus, determination, and effort you are putting forth into reaching your goals and living your best life. As much as we would love life to be predictable and go according to our desired plans, on our time frame, it rarely works out that way. Life is almost never black and white with a 100% chance of sun. The truth is that life is most often gray, it can be a bit muddy at times, and there may be times that the storms you are facing are like nothing you have ever experienced. No matter how hard we try to control situations and outcomes, there will be times when things just do not go according to plan. There will be plot twists, unexpected curveballs, influences, or actions from others, that we have no control over. We will be exhausted, get frustrated, lose hope, want to give up and quit. Our faith will be tested, and at times, shake us to the very core. And that is okay. It is human. You are human.

Some of the most significant moments of my life have been the gray moments and the times when the storm seemed to be completely unbearable. When I look back at those moments, as hard as they were, they are where I have grown the most, where I have had to really look within at what it is that is important to me, what my core values are, and what it is that I need to do to persevere and keep moving forward. It is where I learned to trust and have faith in myself that I would get through whatever it was that I was facing. My efforts, determination, and continued strength would eventually pay off, that I would pull through to see and enjoy those sunny days ahead.

During those gray moments, when you start to doubt and question yourself, and your crown is feeling so heavy that all you want is to cast it aside and give up, take a deep breath. Readjust and refocus on what is in your control, what you can influence, and what or who may be causing you pain or getting in the way. Take a moment to look at all that you have accomplished and overcome. Take a moment to celebrate your strength, your resilience, and the determination that has carried you through, gotten you to where you are and will get you to where you are going. Straighten your crown, hold your head high, and remember that you can, and you will, because you are a badass like that.

"People do not give themselves enough credit
for overcoming things and getting better.
You made it this far. Celebrate your strength."

– Unknown

"I hope that you appreciate yourself
for how far you've already come.
For how graceful you carry yourself
through the different seasons of your life.
For the strength you held yourself with
through every challenge that you had to face.
For the hope you kept up in uncertain times."

– Unknown

"Remember, there's no success without adversity.
The pain of growth should never outweigh the achievements of your success.
Keep going, and through your efforts,
you will reap the rewards you are undoubtedly due.
As you progress, take some time to look back and reflect.
Be critical of your mistakes,
but also proud of your achievements."

– J. Lloyd

A Stronger You
"There will be many things in life that you won't have control over.
They will cripple you, hurt you, break you into pieces,
but they will also build your character, change you completely as a person.
So when you encounter them, don't fear them.
Welcome them as opportunities to grow, to be a better version of you.
You will be hurt but in the same process
you will learn how to find a stronger you."

– POETRY OF DHIMAN

"Do not get impatient or frustrated at every bump.
Breathe. Handle this from a sense of strength.
Trust it will turn out well in time."

– BRENDON BURCHARD

"Do not forget that you're human.
It is okay to have a meltdown. Just don't unpack and live there.
Cry it out and then re-focus on
where you were headed."

– UNKNOWN

"Sometimes you get what you want.
Other times, you get a lesson in patience, timing,
alignment, empathy, compassion, faith, perseverance,
resilience, humility, trust, meaning,
awareness, resistance, purpose, clarity, grief,
beauty and life. Either way, you win."

– Brianna Wiest

"It's always better to be exhausted from little bits of effort, learning, and growth
than to be tired of sitting around doing absolutely nothing.
Progress, no matter how small, feels good.
Take a moment to appreciate the tiny steps you have taken
and how far you have come."

– Marcandangel

"You don't have to solve your whole life overnight.
And you don't have to feel ashamed for being where you are.
All you must focus on is one small thing you can do today
to get closer to where you want to be.
Slowly, one step at a time.
You can get there."

– Daniell Koepke

Note to self:
"Breathe. Be where you are.
You are supposed to be here at this moment.
There is a time and a place for everything, and every step is necessary.
Just keep doing your best, and don't force
what's not yet supposed to fit into your life.
When it's meant to be, it will be."

– Marcandangel

"When life gives you rainy days, wear cute boots and jump in the puddles."

– Unknown

Life Isn't Always Fair
"No matter what it throws your way,
no matter how unfair it may seem,
refuse to play the victim. Refuse to be
ruled by fear, pessimism, and negativity.
Refuse to quit. Be a warrior and work
through whatever life tosses your way
with courage, love, and positivity, and
continually push forward. Because you
are a survivor of the unfairness of life.
You are stronger than you think. And
you are capable of achieving far
more than you believe."

– Unknown

"You're unbelievable.
You put in all this effort day in and day out, then you get
frustrated with yourself because you base your level of success
strictly on your results. You know by now that every single
manifestation, big or small, financial, or physical or mental,
goes through a process—some faster than others.
And as long as you show up for yourself, you'll get close every single time.
The universe always meets your effort halfway.
Let's pivot from 'Why hasn't this happened yet?'
to 'I'm so proud of myself for showing up until it does.'
Divine timing is real. Trust it.
Trust you."

– SOURCE MESSAGES

"Give yourself love.

Give yourself compassion and kindness.

Life can be strange and difficult and beyond your understanding some days.

But it is still beautiful and worthy and there are still reasons for you to keep going anyway.

Even if you do not know the purpose of certain things that have happened to you along the way.

Trust that one day it will make sense.

Maybe your life will not change all of the sudden,

but that doesn't mean that what you are going through will never change.

Give life the time it needs to prepare you for better things.

Give your heart the time it needs to grow through these circumstances."

– Poetry of Dhiman

For You
"This is for the ones who are struggling right now.
This is for the ones who have been having a rough day or week or even year.
The ones who feel like this storm will never end.
Keep fighting for you. Not for your friends, not for your family, but for you.
Keep fighting because deep down, you hold a tiny voice
that knows you were meant for far more than the sadness and pain you are feeling.
Keep fighting because the person you will be on the other side of all this
is cheering for you so much.
Keep fighting because you will get there. And it will be worth it."

– Nikki Banas

"I hope you will walk on this journey knowing that you belong.
I hope even if things sometimes do not go your way,
you will not stop trying, you will not give up on yourself,
and on your toughest days, I hope you will keep reminding yourself of this;
you are loved and you are worthy,
even when it doesn't feel that way."

– POETRY OF DHIMAN

"If your path demands you walk through hell, walk as if you own the place."

– Unknown

"Sometimes instead of saying, 'Just keep a positive mindset,'
what we need to hear is,
'I know this f*cking sucks right now, but you are a badass,
and you're going to push through it.
This moment will make you better.'"

– HANNAH BLUM

"Shout out to everyone making progress
that no one recognizes because you never let anyone see your darkest moments.
You've been silently winning battles and transforming yourself.
Be proud of every step you're making in the right direction.
Keep going because you got this."

– UNKNOWN

"Sometimes, you just have to give yourself a pep talk.
Like hello, you are a badass. Keep your head up; you're doing great.
Love you."

– Unknown

"You really do not realize how brilliantly beautiful you are,
breaking old beliefs and grasping your bliss.
I realize it is ridiculously hard and messy,
but you can do ridiculously hard and messy things.
Are you shaken? Good. Keep going.
You were shaken before, and here you are.
Still standing. Doing this.
Shining and expanding and gloriously undefined."

– Victoria Erickson

"I need you to know something-
That when you're feeling defeated,
beat up and down on your luck,
when you feel like you haven't done
anything or enough,
that the most important things in life cannot be built with your hands.
And even on days you feel burnt out,
dim in the darkness lacking sheen,
I need you to know-
You're still the brightest damn thing I've ever seen."

– AMANDA TORRONI

"Your light is seen, your heart is known,
your soul is cherished by more people than you might imagine.
If you knew how many others have been touched in wonderful ways by you,
you would be astonished.
If you knew how many people feel so much for you, you would be shocked.
You are far more wonderful than you think you are.
Rest with that. Rest easy with that. Breathe again.
You are doing fine. More than fine. Better than fine.
You're doing great.
So relax and love yourself today."

– Neale Donald Walsch

"Chin up, beautiful. You are not struggling. You're merely mid-conquer."

– Unknown

"Message to past self:
I am sorry for not always believing in your potential.
I often held you back with negative thinking and self-doubt
in the most crucial of times when you needed as much positivity as possible,
I didn't always help. But most importantly, I'm thankful for you.
I'm learning so much from watching you through my memories.
Even in the world-ending fears and circumstances, you held to faith and purpose.
You always took that step forward and believed in the bigger picture.
Your faith saved me, and who I am today is thankful that we never gave up.
Love, Self"

–Vybe Source

"Heavy is the crown and yet she wears it as if it were a feather.
There is strength in her heart, determination in her eyes
and the will to survive resides in her soul.
She is you.
A warrior, a champion, a fighter,
a queen."

– R.H. Sin

12
Sprinkle Kindness Like Confetti

Years ago, I was picking up my dry cleaning and the young lady behind the counter, probably in her early twenties, said to me that she had told her mother that she hopes to be like me when she grows up.

I was incredibly touched and honestly a little surprised and confused as to why. I asked her why she felt that way. She shared that out of all the women that came in there, I was one of the only ones that said hello to her and asked about her day. She continued to share that although she was at first intimidated by how confident and put together I seemed when she first met me, she had started looking forward to when I came in because of the conversations we had.

As I drove home, I thought of how that was one of the nicest compliments anyone had ever given me and how significant something as simple as asking about another person's day and showing genuine interest can be. It was something so simple that cost nothing and took little time yet impacted someone so much. It made me wonder how often we have the opportunity to impact someone's life without even realizing we are doing it—often by just a quick hello and, "How are you doing today?"

Think of all the simple and random interactions you have with people throughout your day that may seem insignificant at the time. How often do our natural tendencies to look away, focus on what we are doing or where we need to be get in the way of just saying hello, holding the door for the person behind us, or complimenting someone for something we notice and appreciate? And how often we have the opportunity to impact someone else's day, no matter how insignificant it may seem.

"Some stranger somewhere
still remembers you because you were kind to them
when no one else was."

– Unknown

"You might think that you do not matter in this world,
but because of you,
someone has a favorite mug to drink their tea out of that you bought them.
Someone hears a song on the radio, and it reminds them of you.
Someone has read a book you recommended to them and gotten lost in the pages.
Someone has remembered a joke that you told them and smiled to themselves.
Never think you do not have an impact.
Your fingerprints cannot be wiped away from the little marks of kindness
that you've left behind."

– Unknown

"Think you can't change the world?
Too late, you already have. It was changed for the better the minute you were born.
There are more people than you can imagine who will never be the same
because they came in contact with you,
if only for a fleeting moment."

– GAIL PURCELL ELLIOTT

"You look in the mirror and sometimes see a mess of a human being.
But you don't see the lives you have touched or the people you have saved.
You don't see all the love you've given freely
or the extraordinary memories you have made.
You are a book of beautiful moments and feelings."

– Unknown

"You cannot get through a single day without having an impact on the world around you. What you do makes a difference, and you have to decide what kind of difference you want to make."

– JANE GOODALL

"It is still amazing to me how tenacious our self-doubt patterns are, and yet how quickly our positive self-thoughts can evaporate. This is the stage of the collective unconscious, one where many of us are more inclined to hide our light under a bushel of shame than to celebrate our magnificence. What this tells me is that we have lots of work left to do internally, and just as importantly, that we need to make a point of validating others whenever possible: I love you, you are fantastic, I appreciate what is unique about you, I am grateful for your presence, you rock, etc. There can never be too much kindness, too much attunement, too much honoring of the other. Love them forward…."

– JEFF BROWN

"Kindness begins with the understanding that we all struggle."

– CHARLES GLASSMAN

"You don't have to move mountains.
Simply fall in love with life. Be a tornado of happiness, gratitude, and acceptance.
You will change the world just by being a warm,
kindhearted human being."

– Anita Krizzen

"If you see someone falling behind, walk beside them.
If you see someone being ignored, include them.
If someone has been knocked down, lift them up.
Always remind people of their worth.
One small act could mean the world to them."

– UNKNOWN

"I truly appreciate kindness.
I appreciate people checking up on me.
I appreciate a quick message.
I appreciate those who ask if I'm okay.
I appreciate every single person in my life who has tried to brighten my days.
It's the little things that matter the most."

– Unknown

"Build someone up.
Put their insecurities to sleep. Remind them they are worthy.
Tell them they are incredible.
Be a light in a too often dim world."

– Unknown

"Sometimes all that's needed to light someone's entire day,
to renew their hope in humanity, to give them energy and strength,
is a simple nod, a kind word, a genuine smile.
Be that light."

– BRENDON BURCHARD

"Be the reason someone feels welcomed, seen, heard, valued, loved, and supported."

– Unknown

"Do things for people not because of who they are
or what they do in return but because of who you are."

– Unknown

"Remember whenever you are in a position to help someone,
be glad and always do it because that's the universe
answering someone else's prayers through you."

– Unknown

"Kindness:
Loaning someone your strength
instead of reminding them of their weakness."

– Andy Stanley

"The kindest people are not born that way, they are made. They are the souls that have experienced so much at the hands of life, they are the ones who have dug themselves out of the dark, who have fought to turn every loss into a lesson. The kindest people do not just exist, they choose to soften where circumstance has tried to harden them, they choose to believe in goodness because they have seen firsthand why compassion is so necessary. They have seen firsthand why tenderness is so important in this world"

– UNKNOWN

"She's an angel
who is the essence of compassion
because she knows better than anyone
what it is like to fly with
broken wings.

– JM Storm

"If you have been brutally broken
but still have the courage to be gentle to other living beings,
then you are a badass with
a heart of an angel."

– Keanu Reeves

"She didn't have to stay kind in such a cruel world,
and she didn't have to keep loving after being hurt,
but she did.
I think that is what made her brave."

– Stephanie Bennett-Henry

"What made her brave is how she never stopped being there for other people even when she was struggling with her own issues.
She was fighting for her own life, still stepping up, going to the wall for others, while never saying a word about the war she was losing.
She didn't want to be remembered for her own battle, she wanted to be remembered for simple things like making someone smile or giving someone hope.
She wanted more than anything to leave you a little better than you were before. I hope she did."

– STEPHANIE BENNETT-HENRY

"When our time on earth is done,
money or material things will not matter.
But the love, time, and kindness we have given others
will shine and live on forever."

– Unknown

13

Did You Just Call Me Pretty?

I have never understood how, at times, women can be so unkind to one another—and for no other reason than they feel intimidated, threatened, or insecure because of another woman's beauty, success, personality, or circumstance. We start to compare all that they are or what we perceive them to be to all that we are and what we believe ourselves to be. And it is no wonder, given all the high expectations and pressures we put on ourselves, the unrealistic beliefs and ideas of what beauty is and isn't, and what we define as being "successful" in life. I do not think we realize just how unkind words impact a person and how long they stay with them, even though we are experts at focusing on one little negative when there are 100 positives we could be celebrating. Why, then, would something hurtful or negative that we say not impact another? And maybe that is the end goal. And if so, that is even more sad.

I have been on the receiving end of a lot of hurtful comments by women. Some from women I know and others from women I don't. It took me years to realize that when someone does this to me, often it is not that there is an issue with me. Rather, it has to do with something they are struggling with. But knowing that does not make it any easier or any less hurtful.

My sister and I have discussed this a lot over the years and decided that when someone says something rude or mean to us that was uncalled for, we would simply reply, "Did you just call me pretty?" It always throws the person off, keeps you from lowering yourself to that level, and helps in understanding that there is something personal they are struggling with.

So, the next time someone is rude, simply reply, "Did you just call me pretty?" Not only will you feel better, but chances are, they may feel better as well.

"You're going to meet people who are intimidated by you.
You're different.
People don't know how to react or how to accept someone who doesn't follow the crowd.
They are not used to someone who doesn't try to fit in.
So instead of bolstering your uniqueness,
they'll try to make you feel like you're weird or damaged.
I'm here to offer some well-earned advice:
Screw them."

– ALFA

"People get scared when you try to do something,
especially when it looks like you're succeeding.
People do not get scared when you're failing. It calms them.
But when you are winning, it makes them feel like they're losing,
or worse yet, maybe they should've tried to do something too,
but now it's too late. And since they didn't, they want to stop you.
You can't let them."

– MINDY KALING

"Some people will never like you because your spirit irritates their demons."

– Denzel Washington

"Your truth will bring out the worst in others.
Your love will tingle what they've numbed.
Your authenticity will provoke closed minds.
Your gratitude will irritate trolls.
Your success will attract haters.
Your empowerment will create enemies.
Your uniqueness will antagonize assholes.
Your courage will out cowards.
Your sexuality will freak others out.
Your joy will expose inner shit.
Your compassion will unmask envy.
And love, that's what it's all meant to do.
Your aliveness will reveal many mental prisons
but help to set even more minds free."

– Tanya Markul

"You must understand they fear you.
There is nothing scarier than a girl who knows the power of her flames."

– Nikita Gill

"They are scared of women like you.
Women with hearts big enough to house suitcases full of pain.
Women with laughs so therapeutic they can heal wounds.
Women with passion fierce enough to start wildfires.
They are scared of what they can't tame or understand."

– Billy Chapata

"Strange, isn't it?
You know yourself better than anyone else,
yet you crumble at the words of someone who has not even lived
a second of your life. Focus on your own voice; it is the only one that matters."

– Unknown

"If my strength intimidates you,
if mocking me makes you feel stronger,
if my happiness breaks your spirit….
that's a reflection of your weakness not mine.
I will never allow myself to
be defined by someone's opinion.
Truth is, small minds
can't comprehend big spirits.
My light shines brighter,
my frequency vibrates higher,
and I will not dim my light so you
can feel higher."

– Ivonne Echeve

"Don't personalize or internalize other people's behavior.
What they do is not a reflection of you.
Their actions represent them and where they are in their growth.
Just observe instead of getting caught up
and overreacting emotionally."

– IDIL AHMED

"And the dandelion does not stop growing because it is told that it is a weed.
The dandelion does not care what others see.
It says, 'One day, they'll be making wishes on me.'"

– B. Atkinson

"No one can dictate what attitude you will wear today.
If you meet someone whose intent is to put you down,
remember that it is you who wears the crown."

– DODINSKI

"When you know your worth,
no one can make you feel worthless."

– Unknown

"Do not let the ugly in others kill the beauty in you."

– Unknown

"People will throw stones at you.
Don't throw them back.
Collect them all and build an empire."

– Unknown

"I have battled my whole life to become the strong woman I am today.
If you think you can take me down after all that I have already been through,
give it your best shot. You will never succeed."

– Unknown

"It's a hard truth,
but you'll learn that some people stop liking you when you start outshining them.
And that's when you learn about fake people and which kind you are.
As for me, I know there is enough light for everyone.
I'll even step aside and let you stand in mine so you can shine.
You don't have to root for me, but like it or not,
I am always rooting for you.
That's who I am."

– Stephanie Bennett-Henry

"I forgive you for treating me the way you felt about yourself."

– Butterflies Rising

14

The "No Panties Left Behind" Tribe

When I was going through my divorce and my marriage counselor was encouraging me to "let people in," one of the realizations I had was that I had very few true friends. I decided I needed to work on that—not only building friendships but being a better friend to those around me. I thought of the women I knew, most of whom were professional peers, and thought of those I respected and wanted to get to know better. I started setting up opportunities to have coffee and lunch with them.

On one particular occasion, another woman and I decided to set up a time for a girls' day to make vision boards. We thought of a handful of women that we both knew and wanted to get to know better and invited them to participate with us. We got together on a Saturday morning with piles of old magazines, photos, inspirational quotes, and plenty of food to munch on. We sat around the table working on our vision boards, enjoying one another's company, while we learned things about each other that we never knew.

While I was flipping through a magazine, I found an ad for tampons with the slogan, "No Panties Left Behind." When the lady next to me was up getting some food, I cut out the slogan and set it on her vision board. It took her a while to find it, but when she did, we both could not stop laughing, and she decided it had to stay. That day turned out to be so significant and empowering for all of us, and we all walked away realizing how much we needed that time and support from one another. We decided that we needed to be a tribe for one another, and that was the moment The "No Panties Left Behind" Tribe was born.

We got together on occasion to have a glass of wine or lunch with one another, and it became a place where we could be open, honest, and real amongst friends. One time, when we were planning to meet for a glass of wine, we decided we needed to invite another woman who had not been there on Vision Board Day. That night, she shared with us that she was moving out of state and how much it meant to her to be included because everyone knew that we were "the cool kids."

Hmmm. I had no idea that people thought of me as one of the cool kids, especially since I grew up never being one of the cool kids. I wanted to do something for her to remind her that she would always be a member of The "No Panties Left Behind" Tribe.

That gave me the idea to make official framed certificates for all of us for Christmas that year that stated:

This certifies that you are an official member of The "No Panties Left Behind" Tribe. This membership includes, but is not limited to, the following: Unwavering support and friendship, unconditional love and acceptance, unscrupulous shenanigans, uninhibited laughter, often caused by inappropriate humor and positive cheer, and complete confidentiality in regard to any conversations or moments shared together amongst tribe members.

It was a silly and fun gesture for the women who had come into my life and had become part of my "tribe," and it also made me think about how I always wanted to be included growing up and how that doesn't ever change as we get older. Just as much as we were all needing supportive and trusting friends, so were so many other women all around us.

To this day, my framed "No Panties Left Behind" certificate still hangs in my office and has become a reminder to me that all of us need to feel supported, included, encouraged, and empowered by one another and we, as women, need to become a tribe of one.

SHINE ON, YOU CRAZY DIAMOND

"The right people will find you.
They will speak to you differently. They will inspire you.
They will motivate you. They will help you heal.
Help you learn new things about yourself. Discover the deeper parts within.
The right people will make you feel at home.
And you will never have to worry about them saying goodbye.
You will know who they are."

– R.M. Drake

"Celebrate the people in your life who are there because they love you for no other reason than because you are you."

– Unknown

"A true friend doesn't care if you're broke, upset,
what you are wearing, if your house is a mess,
or if your family is filled with crazy people.
They love you for who you are."

– Unknown

"When you find people who not only tolerate your quirks,
but celebrate them with glad cries of, 'Me too,'
be sure to cherish them.
Because those weirdos are your tribe."

– Sweatpants and Coffee

"Be with the sassy girls.
The ones with brilliant minds, bare feet,
sweet hearts, and feisty spirits,
and who live for doing what they've
been told is impossible."

– UNKNOWN

"Be around the light bringers,
the magic makers, the world shifters, the game-changers.
They challenge you, break you, open you, and lift you up.
They don't let you play small with your life.
These are your people.
This is your tribe."

– Unknown

"Choose to be in the company of those who hold a space for you to achieve the joy of maximizing rather than minimizing your highest human potential."

– Dr. Wayne Dyer

"Surround yourself with people who clearly love your light and add to it."

– KAREN SALMANSOHN

"You'll know the people that feed your soul
because you'll feel good after spending time with them."

– LATIKA TEOTIA

"The circles of women around us
weave invisible webs of love that carry us
when we are weak and sing with us
when we are strong."

– SARK

"Your friends are your release.
They're who you have the most fun with,
and yet when the going gets tough,
those people turn around, and suddenly they're not just making you laugh,
they are being this rock and giving you their advice.
Even though you are so much your own person,
if you dissect yourself, I guarantee you,
your friends are in there.
Their influence is incredible."

– Unknown

"Friendship is not just a word or some kind of liability.
It is a silent promise that I was, I am,
and I will always be there for you."

– Unknown

"Behind every successful woman is a tribe of other successful women who have her back."

– UNKNOWN

"Be that girl who roots for the other girl,
tells a stranger her hair looks amazing,
and encourages other women to believe in themselves
and their dreams."

– Unknown

"Be a woman other women can trust.
Have the courage to tell another woman directly when she has offended,
hurt, or disappointed you.
Successful women have a tribe of loyal and honest women behind them.
Not haters. Not backstabbers or women who whisper behind their back.
Be a woman who loves other women."

– Sophie A. Nelson

"Imagine a community of women inspiring
its daughters, granddaughters, and nieces
to refuse to twist their lives out of shape to fit into expectations,
supporting them to refuse to please others
by pretending to be less intelligent and gifted than they are,
and empowering them to love their woman-bodies regardless.
Imagine yourself as part of this community."

– Patricia Lynn Reilly

"I think women are powerful, and I think we're more powerful together than separate."

– Zendaya Coleman

15

When I Grow Up, I Want to Be Wonder Woman

The first book I ever wrote was when I was in kindergarten. It was titled **All About Catherine**. In it, I drew pictures of my family, my house, and of myself. I said, *"Please do not serve me eggs,"* and *"When I grow up, I want to be Wonder Woman."* All these years later, I still don't really care for eggs, and I still want to be Wonder Woman when I grow up.

The idea of being Wonder Woman has always been more of a mindset and an attitude for me. Don't get me wrong. I still would love to rock the outfit while cruising in the invisible plane. Being Wonder Woman is a belief in myself, a level of confidence I have always had, knowing that I am capable of doing anything I set my mind to, no matter how difficult. It is about integrity, truth, honesty, excellence, walking the walk, and serving others.

My most cherished gifts have been the homemade, personal gifts that my daughter has made me throughout her life. One of the most touching and special gifts she ever gave me is one she made for me for Mother's Day when she was in college. It's a shadow box with a female superhero action figurine standing next to a piece of paper where she wrote:

Reasons why my mother is my hero:

If she wants something, she gets that shit done! *She gave sickness the middle finger and got super healthy and buff, now she can beat up all y'all's mom. * She is literally a Barbie doll. *She reached the top but refuses to stop. * She is the best person to be a goofball with. *She believes in my potential more than anyone else. * She accepts and loves everyone. * "Classic Catherine." *She wants to be Wonder Woman, but she left WW in the dust decades ago. *My mom is more powerful, more beautiful, and more amazing. *She is my favorite superhero! *

I believe there is a Wonder Woman in all of us. We find her when we discover, develop, and confidently and unapologetically use our talents, abilities, and purpose to do and be our best, and she shines brightest when we encourage, uplift, and support others. She is the woman who appears when we embody all that is right and good in the world with hearts that are honest, compassionate, filled with love, and of service to those in need.

"Wonder Woman is not a fictional character. Wonder Woman is a mindset."

– UNKNOWN

"Nobody has the power to stop what you have been blessed with."

– Unknown

"Be not afraid of greatness.
Some are born great, some achieve greatness,
and some have greatness
thrust upon them."

– William Shakespeare

"Don't let anything stop you from chasing your own greatness."

– Unknown

"I was born with something inside me
that refuses to settle for average.
I do not know what it is,
but I am grateful I have it."

– UNKNOWN

Warrior

"Be a warrior. Fight for what you believe in and never, ever hold back.

Firstly, go toward your dreams with boldness and be blessed.

Hold your ground in the face of conflict. Knock barriers down with courage and grace.

Do not give up when you find yourself face to face with an obstacle,

instead continue forward with abandon.

Keep the fire in your heart burning strong, and do not ever let your flame fade away.

Remind yourself that what you are fighting for is worth it.

And remember that you will overcome everything that comes your way,

because my beautiful friend,

you are a warrior."

– Nikki Banas

"Never bend your head.
Hold it high. Look at the world straight in the eyes."

– Unknown

"Put your hand on your heart," the old man said.

Inside you there is a power, there are ideas, thoughts that no one has ever thought of,

there is the strength to love, purely and intensely,

and to have someone love you back.

There is the power to make people happy and to make people laugh.

It's for compliments and the power to change lives and futures.

Don't forget that power,

and don't ever give up on it."

– ATTICUS

"Visualize your highest self, then start showing up as her."

– Unknown

Note to self:
"The world needs you to show up today.
You are powerful, you are valuable,
and what you believe changes the world."

– Unknown

"She is what the world loves to hate:
pure, authentic, tested, and brave.
And that is why her kind
will save this world."

– Unknown

"No one is born a warrior.
You choose to be one when you refuse to stay seated.
You choose to be one when you refuse to back down.
You choose to be one when you stand up after getting knocked down.
You choose to be one, because if not you, who?"

– Being Caballero

"To be a warrior is not a simple matter of wishing to be one.
It is rather an endless struggle that will go on to the very last moment of our lives.
Nobody is born a warrior
in the same way that nobody is born an average person.
We make ourselves into one or the other."

– CARLOS CASTANEDA

"You didn't wake up today to be mediocre."

– Unknown

"I think it is possible for ordinary people to choose to be extraordinary."

– Elon Musk

"The sooner you believe that you are extraordinary,
the sooner others will follow."

– Joyce Chang

"She has got that whole purpose-driven,
warrior princess,
save-the-world type vibe."

– Unknown

"I want to be the girl who changed everything.
The girl who made a difference.
The girl who gave you a story to tell."

– Unknown

"There is no limit to what we as women can accomplish."

– Michelle Obama

"I figure if a girl wants to be a legend, she should go ahead and be one."

– Calamity Jane

16

Put On Your Big Girl Pants and Be Your Own Hero

I didn't finish college. When I was single and pregnant with my daughter, I swore I would go back to school when she was one. And as it goes, life happens, there were bills to pay, and years later, that college degree is still sitting there on my bucket list. It bothered me for years that I could not put that on my resume, even though I always had the confidence and belief that I was capable, had the talent and work ethic to do any job, and have continued to grow and advance in my career with many incredible opportunities and amazing accomplishments. Many times, people (and even myself in the past) have let certain expectations of what people think makes someone deserving of something keep them from really going after what they want.

I was having a conversation with a co-worker discussing advancement, taking risks, and how if you are unhappy, making a change. She said to me, "Not everybody is like you. Not everyone can just decide they want to do something and then go do it."

I replied, "You know, you're right. You are not like me. You have a college degree. You have done all the things that most companies look for when hiring a candidate. The difference between you and me is that I have this belief and confidence in myself that I'm capable and deserving of anything I set my mind to. You just need to believe that you can do it, whatever it is you want to do, and then go do it."

"Be your own hero" has always been something that has just resonated with me to my very core. It is believing in yourself and knowing that you are worthy of whatever it is that you want to do and be and that you can accomplish anything you set your mind to. It is about taking risks and ridding yourself of the limitations you have created in your mind. It's about having dreams and continually learning new things.

It's about not sitting back and waiting on others to make it happen. It's a willingness to get out of your comfort zone and do whatever it takes to make it happen regardless of how scared you are and how impossible it seems. It's about focusing on all that can go right instead of all that could possibly go wrong. It's about refusing to give up despite the difficulties and trusting and having faith in your abilities. It's about being self-sufficient and realizing that nobody owes you anything.

Take responsibility and stop making excuses. Commit yourself to work toward it. Work hard. Do not be afraid of the time or effort needed to accomplish something. It is in the journey and the process that you will learn and develop your talents, strengths, and character. Be crazy enough to believe you will succeed. Set goals and celebrate every small success that gets you one step closer to what you are striving for.

Yes, things happen in life that are out of your control, and you have the power to control how you react to those situations and how you will use them to move forward. Decide to let those moments in your life be launching pads and opportunities for growth. Regardless of how painful, disappointing, or unfair they may be. Focus on having the mindset that challenges are opportunities, and the greater the challenge, the greater the opportunity. Accept that you won't always have the luxury of believing in or depending on other people. You do, however, always have the luxury of believing in and being able to depend on yourself if you choose to—if you allow yourself to.

"Everything you do is based on the choices you make.
It's not your parents, your past relationships, your job,
the economy, the weather, an argument, or your age that is to blame.
You, and only you, are responsible for every decision and choice you make.
Period."

– Wayne Dyer

"Life isn't always fair.
Some people are born into better environments,
some have better genetics, and some are in the right place at the right time.
If you're trying to change your life, all this is irrelevant.
All that matters is that you accept where you are,
figure out where you want to be,
and then do what you can today
and every day to hold your head high
and keep moving forward."

– UNKNOWN

"You don't have a right to the cards you believe you should have been dealt. You have an obligation to play the hell out of the ones you're holding."

– Cheryl Strayed

"Sis, you're over here doubting yourself while
so many people are afraid of your potential.
Get it together."

– Unknown

"Stop letting your potential go to waste
because you don't feel confident or ready enough.
People with half your talent are making serious waves
while you're still waiting to feel ready."

– UNKNOWN

"The only thing standing between you and your goal
is the bullshit story you keep telling yourself
as to why you can't achieve it."

– The Wolf of Wall Street

"You can't be committed to your own bullshit and to your growth.
It's one or the other."

– Scott Stabile

"To attract better you have to become better yourself.
You can't do the same things and expect change. You can't blame anyone or anything.
It's time to take responsibility for your reality. Start transforming your mindset. Start upgrading your habits. Start being more positive."

– Idil Ahmed

"You always knew that one day you would stand up for yourself.
That one day, you would raise the standard of your life.
That one day, you would say to yourself, 'Enough with this bullshit.'
You might as well make today that day."

– STEVE MARABOLI

"There is hoping your life will improve, and then there is the fire,
a deep obsession to change and become better,
to forge a vibrant and abundant life by sheer will,
daily focus, and struggle, and the guts to push yourself,
lift yourself up, adapt, persist
and to be extraordinary."

– BRENDON BURCHARD

"Almost every successful person begins with two beliefs.
The future can be better than the present,
and I have the power to make it so."

– Unknown

"Successful people are 100% convinced that they are masters of their own destiny. They're not creatures of circumstance. If the circumstances around them suck, they change them."

– Jordan Belfort

"You're never going to be 100% ready
and it's never going to be just the right time,
but that's the point.
It means that every moment is also the right moment,
if you want it, you just have to do it."

– Unknown

"Start now.
Start where you are. Start with fear.
Start with pain. Start with doubt. Start with hands shaking.
Start with voice trembling but start.
Start and don't stop.
Start where you are with what you have…
Just start."

– Unknown

"Sometimes the smallest step in the right direction
ends up being the biggest step of your life.
Tiptoe if you must but take the step."

– Unknown

"She was never quite ready,
but she was brave,
and the universe listens to brave."

– Rebecca Ray

"There is a powerful moment in life when you either decide to tolerate life the way it is or decide to be brave and change it."

– Rachel Marie Martin

"The willingness to show up changes us.
It makes us a little braver each time."

– Brene Brown

"Her courage was her crown, and she wore it like a queen."

– ATTICUS

"Hard times don't create heroes.
It is during the hard times when the hero
within us is revealed."

– BOB RILEY

"Perfect and bulletproof are seductive,
but they don't exist in the human experience.
We must walk into the arena, whatever it may be,
a new relationship, an important meeting, or creative process,
or difficult family conversations,
with courage and the willingness to engage,
rather than sitting on the sidelines and hurling judgment and advice.
We must dare to show up and let ourselves be seen.
This is vulnerability.
This is daring greatly."

– BRENE BROWN

"There is a huge superhero in all of us.
We just need the courage to put on the cape."

– SUPERMAN

"Crowns aren't made of rhinestones.
They are made of discipline, determination,
and hard to find alloy called courage."

– Unknown

"There is one grand lie—that we are limited.
The only limits we have are the limits we believe."

– DR. WAYNE DYER

"Believe in your own potential. You are capable of great transformations. You have become so many versions of yourself over the years. There is still so much for you to discover about yourself. Do not give up on you. Let your dreams shift and change. Let your ambitions rise and fall. But don't stop believing in your capacity for growth. It is not time for you to whittle your desires down to regrets. Experiment. Shift. Pivot. Be flexible in your identity. This world can be very difficult, but please don't be your own biggest barrier. Do not be the person who tells you that you can't do it, or it's too late, or you're too old. You can do it. It's not too late. And age does not tell you what's possible for you. Wherever you are now, you can be in a totally different place in a month, a year from now. So much can change when you stay *open*. When you stay *hopeful*. Stop resisting life and the changes it wants from you. Let life take you on the tide for a while. See where you go. See all that is available for you when you are open to transformation."

– Jamie Varon

"If the only challenges you are facing in life right now are the ones life has thrown at you, then you are not directing your own destiny – you are merely reacting to the world. You are not guiding yourself. The greatest challenges we face in life should be the ones we decide to take on because we have bold vision for ourselves. That is how you know you are consciously designing your life."

– Brendon Burchard

"When we demand of ourselves
to rise to another level of service and energy in the world,
everybody feels it.
And that's what changes the world.
A different level of energy from us."

– BRENDON BURCHARD

"If we did the things we are capable of, we would astound ourselves."

– Thomas Edison

"It has long since come to my attention that people of accomplishment
rarely sat back and let things happen to them.
They went out and happened to things."

– Leonardo da Vinci

"I stopped waiting for the light at the end of the tunnel and lit that bitch up myself."

– Unknown

"Write your own part.
It is the only way I've gotten anywhere.
It is much harder work,
but sometimes, you have to take destiny into your own hands.
It forces you to think about what your strengths really are,
and once you find them, you can showcase them,
and no one can stop you."

– Mindy Kaling

"When people ask what you do, answer: 'Whatever it takes.'"

– Unknown

"She was ambitious and knew exactly what she wanted.
She was always mistaken for being too demanding
when she simply knew where she was headed
and wouldn't settle for less.
She wouldn't let anyone dull her shine
because she knew her perseverance would one day
open the door to a brighter future.
Her unflinching determination was a beautiful example
to set for all women to never give up."

– Unknown

"Once in a while, blow your own damn mind."

– Unknown

"She unleashed her inner goddess and
became the woman her soul knew she could be."

– MICHELLE SCHAPER

17

Shine On, You Crazy Diamond

When I was in my late teens, an elderly man approached me and said, "I saw you sitting over here, and I could not stop looking at you because there is a light completely surrounding you." Similar situations have happened at other times in my life as well. At first, I never really thought much of it, but as I got older, and it would happen, I found myself wondering why it was and what caused that light. One thing I did realize is that those moments were times in my life where I was confident in myself and being true to who I am.

There have also been times in my life, with personal and professional relationships, and within my own family, when other people's lack of belief or confidence in themselves caused me to feel as though I need to diminish who I am to accommodate their insecurities, often without even realizing it. I would downplay accomplishments or successes, convince myself that confidence in myself is self-centered. I would find myself almost apologizing or feeling guilty for where I am in my life even though I have put in the blood, sweat, and tears. I reserve excitement, exuberance, and emotion to match the level they are comfortable with. Why? Why do I hold back with reservation, apologize for, downplay, and diminish who I am, what I feel, and what I have accomplished just to make others feel better about who they are and where they are in their own journey? Why do I let others diminish my confidence in who I am? Confidence is one of the most powerful things you have. It is one of the things that no one can take from you, yet it is so powerful that it is often the first thing people will try to diminish or take from you.

Years ago, I accepted a position at a company and immediately felt that one of the women that I worked with did not like me or my positive, confident, and playful energy. She was incredibly quiet and seemed short with me. I decided that even if she didn't like me, I was just going to be me and try to get to know her and become friends with her. About a year later, when I gave notice that I was leaving the company, she pulled me into her office and shared that she felt the reason I had to come to work there was that I was meant to help her gain the confidence and self-esteem she needed to leave an abusive marriage. I did not realize that in such a short time that my befriending her, positive affirmations, encouraging her, simple playful and sarcastic moments, and simply just being true to who I was, would have such an impact on her.

Standing in your light with confidence means being true to who you are without apology, reservation, or hesitation. It is essential not only for you, but your light and who you are can and will impact so many people around you, often without you even realizing it.

"Beautiful girl,
you don't even realize that some people look at your madness
and see nothing but brilliance and grace."

– Stephanie Bennett-Henry

"I wish I could show you when you were lonely or in darkness
the astonishing light of your own being."

– Hafiz

"You are not the darkness you endured,
you are the light that refuses to surrender."

– John Mark Green

"You are a light.
Remember that. Let that sink into your heart, your life.
See what it means and how it feels to live in that truth.
Other people won't be able to help but notice you."

– UNKNOWN

"You are a diamond in the rough,
sweet girl, so tough.
Maybe you'll get scratched through this dark mess,
but remember,
your sparkle will never show any less.
Stay tough and don't ever try
to hide your shine."

– STEPHANIE BENNETT-HENRY

"Your work is to discover who you are
and then with all your heart
give your light to the world."

– Jennifer Williamson

Stars

"Like a beautiful star shining in the night sky,
your purpose is not to compare your light or brightness to any other star.
Your purpose is not to wish you were a moon or a planet
or to wish you were somewhere else.
Your purpose is not to change who you are or what you are made of.
Your purpose is to shine your light as bright and as beautiful as only you can.
Your purpose is to celebrate the light of others
while celebrating your own light
because it is only when we are all shining our own unique lights
that we can light up the entire night sky."

– Nikki Banas

"When you see that the light filtering through the clouds is also in you, you'll know you can't lose what's inside. You can't lose who you are. So let your light shine. Be the sun in someone else's storm. It's part of why you're here.

There's a light buried in your soul. The same light that gives life to everything around you.

When you see yourself in everything, in the light rising through the curtains and the stars studded in the sky, the world is a brighter place.

Things are a little less… dark. You remember how strong and resilient you are. Because: you're life, you're here, and you've got stardust in you.

So when life feels too hard and the world feels hopeless, take heart. The best gift you can give everyone around you is your own courage to shine, to help, to rise, to be true to who you want to be, to love: even still.

Take heart because what's inside is the most powerful force in the universe. Call it light, call it potential, call it whatever feels right to you."

– RUMI

"Our deepest fear is not that we are inadequate.

Our deepest fear is that we are powerful beyond measure.

It is our light, not our darkness, that most frightens us.

We ask ourselves; who am I to be brilliant, gorgeous, talented, fabulous?

Actually, who are you not to be? You are a child of God.

Your playing small does not serve the world.

There is nothing enlightened about shrinking so that other people won't feel insecure.

We are all meant to shine, as children do.

We were born to make manifest the glory of God that is within us.

It's not just in some of us; it's in everyone.

And as we let our own light shine,

we unconsciously give other people permission to do the same.

As we are liberated from our own fear,

our presence automatically liberates others."

– Marianne Williamson

"These facts are directed to you:
Yes, you, the person who is a light
in so many people's lives without knowing.
You are precious, you are great,
you are the one that can make anything happen.
If anyone can change the world
and make it a better place, it's you.
You have a talent, and you should use it.
Never forget that you are special."

– SOULFUL REFLECTIONS

"You are precious and brighter than all light.
You carry wonder in your eyes and beauty in your soul.
You have freedom in your step,
and you don't fear dancing in the rain.
You are light and grace,
you are lovely and free."

– G.C.

The Fire Inside You
"There is enough fire inside you to put all of hell to shame,
but you are pretending to be water
for someone who is too afraid to handle the dragons in your belly.
Stop crushing the thing that makes you.
Embrace the flames.
Be whole again for yourself
and no one else."

– Nikita Gill

"Give yourself permission to sparkle boldly."

– Rhonda Hendricks

"Some people are going to reject you
simply because you shine too bright for them.
That's okay. Keep shining."

– Mandy Hale

"Do not allow others to diminish your light
due to their own fears and insecurities.
Instead, let your light shine so brightly
that you illuminate a pathway
for others to find their way
out of the darkness."

– Dr. Stacey A. Maxwell

"I think the best role models for women
are people who are fruitfully and confidently themselves,
who bring light into the world."

– MERYL STREEP

"She is magic,
because despite her circumstances,
she continues to spread her light,
her truth, and her love."

– ALFA

"My goal in life is to be one of those people who are just light.
You see them and you suddenly feel so warm inside,
and all you want to do is hug them.
And they look at you and smile with the warmest light in their eyes…
And you love them.
Maybe not in a romantic way,
but you just want to be close to them
and you hope some of their light
transfers on to you."

– Unknown

"She'd tried blending in,
and it wasn't working for her because the truth was,
she was born to sparkle."

– QUEENISMS

"Tired of trying to cram her sparkly, star-shaped self
into society's beige square holes,
she chose to embrace her ridiculous awesomeness
and shine like the freaking supernova
she was meant to be."

– Unknown

18

You Can't Keep a Good Woman Down

I have had a few failed marriages. It's something that I have been hard on myself for and something that I have felt shame about. It is also something that I have allowed other people's opinions or comments to seep in and impact my self-worth. I let comments like, "You're just not good at marriage. Maybe you should just not get married again," or "You just aren't good at staying in a relationship" have such a negative impact on my belief in myself. People have said, "Well, at least I have never been divorced," like it was a badge of honor, no matter how bad or unhealthy their relationship was.

I started believing I was successful in all areas of my life, just not love. I started believing that not only was I incapable of loving, but I was also not worthy of finding love again. It was not until I did that exercise of writing out my life story and sharing it with my friend that I let myself look at things differently. When my friend shared that I had been looking at things all wrong, feeling shame and embarrassment instead of being proud of all I have overcome, the light came on.

I thought of my failed marriages and all that played a role in them ending. There were things I had to take responsibility for and many things that were out of my control. And I realized that I do in fact have a huge capacity and ability to love; I just have a low capacity and ability to deal with and accept bullshit.

I was looking at it all wrong. It was not about failed relationships, divorce, or even lack of love. It was about how many times I had the courage to walk away from a situation or person that wasn't safe or healthy. It was about accepting that I deserved better, and I was allowed to put my needs and well-being, and that of my daughter, first. It was about being completely knocked down, yet once again, picking up the pieces of a broken life and building it into something beautiful and worthy of me.

Life happens. Things happen. People and circumstances change. We get dealt a card that we have no idea how to play, and at the same time, we are resilient. We are strong, courageous, capable individuals who cannot and will not be held down. At times it may take longer to get up, sometimes more than others, but what is important is that you get up. You rise. You hold your head high and confidently and unapologetically do what is best for you.

"You can't hold a good woman down.
She can be cheated on, lied to,
taken advantage of by every man she has ever loved,
yet she's the one they miss in the end.
She's the one they swear over for letting go.
She's the one that haunts their thoughts.
She's the one that's gathered all her dignity from their misuse
and went on to love again.
She rises like a phoenix after betrayal,
and damn, she lights up the sky."

– ALFA

"She's dangerous because she knows what it's like to fall
and get back up a thousand times.
Rock bottom knows her name,
and the only person that saved her is her.
She is not afraid of breaking."

– STEPHANIE BENNETT-HENRY

"She will rise.
With a spine of steel and a roar like thunder,
she will rise."

– Nicole Lyons

"She knows who she is,
who she's not,
and who she's never willing to be again.
She spent a lot of time building herself back up
after being torn down
and if there's one thing she knows for sure,
it's that her peace is never something that's up for grabs.
She's worked way too hard
to just let anyone touch it."

– STEPHANIE BENNETT-HENRY

"The devil whispered in my ear,
'You're not strong enough to withstand the storm.'
Today I whispered in the Devil's ear,
'I am the storm.'"

– Unknown

"She stood in the storm
and when the wind did not blow her away,
she adjusted her crown
and kept walking."

– Unknown

"She's been through hell and came out, an angel.
You didn't break her, darling.
You don't own that kind of power."

– BMM Poetry

"I wasn't born with this heart,
I had to venture into hell, more than once,
and come back still wounded
but unbreakable."

– Stephanie Bennett-Henry

"A champion is defined not by their wins
but by how they recover when they fall."

– SERENA WILLIAMS

"Sweet girl,
maybe you don't know yet,
but one day, you will look back at yourself,
at the sadness, the heartbreak,
every moment that did not go as planned,
and you're going to think: Silly girl, you silly, beautiful girl,
you had to go through that. You had to break like that,
you had to fail so many times and crash into rock-bottom,
so you could learn so many things.
Like the grace in the fall, the light at the bottom,
the flip side of the sadness and all the sad songs that helped you feel less alone.
You had to go through that to realize there is strength in the pieces,
courage in the pain, and so much self-discovery
in all the plans that didn't make it.
But mostly, you had to go through that… Sweet, silly, beautiful girl,
to get your footing, learn to fly, and become the strong,
brave, brilliant, warrior of a woman you are now.
Look at you… You're not falling anymore.
It was a long time coming,
but I swear you're smiling when you get here."

– STEPHANIE BENNETT-HENRY

"And despite hitting rock-bottom, you got back up.
When you thought you wouldn't see the light at the end of the tunnel,
you created it.
Your story is one of overcoming.
Please acknowledge how powerful you are."

– ASH ALVES

"Queens will always turn pain into power."

– Unknown

"She never seemed shattered to me;
she was a breathtaking mosaic of the battles she won."

– Matt Baker

"I love the way she survived.
Survival looked good on her.
There were no dark marks under her eyes.
Maybe deep inside,
but I liked the way she looked through them and laughed at life.
She did it gracefully.
She had walked over glass and through fire,
but still smiled, and honestly,
I'm not interested in people who haven't lived and died a few times,
who haven't yet had their hearts ripped out
or know what it feels like to lose everything.
I trust those people because they stand for something.
I knew what she had been through.
I wanted to thank her for surviving
and to know she now had someone
willing to stand with her too."

– J. Raymond Maybe

"Pain shapes a woman into a warrior."

– R.H. Sin

"As the legend goes,
when the Phoenix resurrects from the flames,
she is even more beautiful
than before."

– Unknown

"She is beautiful.
But you really cannot comprehend it
until you understand that she is the result of the pieces
that she refused to let life
take from her."

– J.M. Storm

"The women whom I love and admire for their strength and grace
did not get that way because shit worked out.
They got that way because shit went wrong,
and they handled it.
They handled it in a thousand different ways,
on a thousand different days,
but they handled it.
Those women are my superheroes."

– Unknown

"Now, every time I witness a strong woman,
I want to know: What dark did you conquer in your story?
Mountains do not rise without earthquakes."

– UNKNOWN

"Life tried to crush her
but only succeeded in creating a diamond."

– John Mark Green

"She had a glittering heart of glass
and every time it shattered
you'd see her shining brighter than the last."

– MICHELLE SCHAPER

"Is there anything she can't handle?
She has been broken. She has been knocked down.
She has been defeated.
She has felt the pain that most could not handle.
She looks fear in the face year after year,
day after day, yet she never runs; she never hides.
She always finds a way to get back up.
She is unbreakable. She is a warrior.
She is you."

– Unknown

"And then one day I looked in the mirror and realized, 'Wow.
After all that hurt, and the bruises, and everything I've been through,
I made it. I did it. I survived, and I am stronger.'
So I stood up tall, and I straightened my crown, and I walked away
like the queen that I am."

– Unknown

19

Wear the Crown. Be the Crown. You Are the Crown.

There have been many times throughout my career that a professional peer has come to me and mentioned that I intimidate and scare a lot of the staff. It has always bothered me because I feel that I always try to treat everyone as equals, make a point to say hello to everyone, and try to get to know all of my team members. My intent is always to be the positive, supportive, motivational leader who could have fun while still setting standards for excellence.

One day when I was told that a particular team member was intimidated and scared of me, I decided to go ask her why. Not to embarrass her or make her feel uncomfortable, but to help me better understand so that I could be a better leader. When I asked her why, she hesitated and then shared, "It's just the way you walk in a room and own it. Your confidence in yourself and the way you carry yourself is so noticeable, and it can be a little intimidating." I started to ask the question "why" whenever it came up, and it was always a similar reply. I came to realize I wasn't doing anything wrong, and I also learned just how much our confidence in ourselves and who we are, shows up in all that we do whether we realize it or not.

Believe and have confidence in yourself. Set standards of excellence for yourself. Know and believe in your worth as a woman and human being, and never question the value that you add to those around you. You are a queen. Always wear your crown with confidence and in a way that shows and allows other women to do the same.

"It is not how big you are; it is how big you play."

– Unknown

"Self-confidence is a superpower.
Once you start to believe in yourself,
magic starts happening."

– UNKNOWN

"Self-confidence is the best outfit.
Rock it. Own it."

– Racquel Dorsey

"Know your worth.
It's always a beautiful moment
when you know how much you bring to yourself,
to others, and to the world.
Never let anyone tell you you're less
than the value you know you have."

– UNKNOWN

"I know my worth.
I have paid dearly for every ounce of it."

– Alfa

"Raise your standards.
Raise your expectations.
Raise your minimums of what you will allow into your life
that do not honor or respect you.
Be bold, push the boundaries,
and you will be rewarded."

– Brendon Burchard

"When you are able to maintain your highest standards of integrity,
regardless of what others may do,
you are destined for greatness."

– Napoleon Hill

"Do not lower your standards to keep anyone.
Make them meet you at your level.
Self-respect is power."

– Unknown

"Get honest with people about who you are,
what you want,
and how you expect to be treated.
Standards only scare off people
who are not meant for you."

– Unknown

"Strong women do not have attitudes; they have standards."

– UNKNOWN

"Incredibly powerful women do not explain why they want respect.
They simply do not engage those who do not give it to them."

– Unknown

"Live in such a way that if anyone should speak badly of you,
no one would believe it."

– Unknown

"There will always be someone better than you,
so don't worry about being the best.
Just focus on being the best version of yourself."

– ROGER LEE

"No one is you, and that is your power."

– DAVE GROHL

"My mother told me to be a lady.
And for her, that meant to be your own person.
Be independent."

– Ruth Bader Ginsberg

"Be the strong woman that everyone knew would make it through the fire.
Be the fearless queen who dares to do anything.
Be the independent woman who chooses to have a man in her life
but does not need one.
Be the woman you want to be,
not who everyone tells you to be.
Be you."

– K. MASTERS

"I am different.
Always have been. It took a while,
but I have accepted that I am magic,
not meant for everyone to understand.
So they question. That is okay.
I will stay in my lane being all magical and stuff."

– Unknown

"She's a little bit of sass and a lot of badass."

– Unknown

"She's a balance of strength and femininity.
She's a blend of silly and serious.
She's a dreamer with her feet still on the ground.
The kind of person that can find the sunrise in a rainstorm.
She is a once-in-a-lifetime woman."

– J. Iron Word

"Darling, you've got magic in your bones
and gold in your soul.
Don't let anyone treat you like you're ordinary."

– Iambrillyant

"When you start using your personality
to serve the greater calling that your soul came here for,
nobody can touch you.
Because that is what authentic power is."

– UNKNOWN

"She's the kind of queen who knows her crown isn't on her head but in her soul."

– Unknown

"The empowered woman is powerful beyond measure
and beautiful beyond description."

– Steve Maraboli

"I decided that I wasn't bossy; I was strong.
I wasn't loud; I was a young woman
who has something to say."

– Michelle Obama

"A strong and confident woman
does not walk into a room with her nose in the air,
thinking she is better than everyone else.
She walks into a room not having to compare herself to anyone else.
She is aware of her individuality
and knows of her own worth."

– Unknown

"May your vibes shift the whole damn frequency of the room when you walk in."

– Unknown

"The biggest disservice you can perform in this life is selling yourself short."

– Unknown

"Don't lowball yourself.
If you've done the work and put in the miles and service with excellence,
you're worth more than you probably believe."

– BRENDON BURCHARD

"The whole time you thought you weren't good enough,
you were overqualified."

– SCIENCE OF POSITIVITY

"Be the kind of person who makes other people want to up their game."

– Unknown

"To all the girls who no longer believe
in fairy tales or happy endings,
you are the writer of the story.
Chin up and straighten your crown;
you're the queen of this kingdom
and only you know how to rule it."

– B. DIVINE

Acknowledgements

My daughter Sabrianna- There are no words to truly express all that my heart feels for you and the depths of gratitude I feel every day for the blessing of having you as my daughter and friend.

My husband Marv- Thank you for showing me what it is to truly and unconditionally be loved, accepted, and cherished for the woman that I am. Your constant support, encouragement, and the love and friendship we share, are treasures I cherish. You hold my heart.

To the women in my life, both family and friends- For all the ways you touch my life that you may never know about or realize, I thank you. Your friendship, your light, your kindness and compassion, your humor and grace, determination and strength, are felt and have such an impact in helping me continue to grow into the woman that I am.

To Kelli and Greg- Thank you for believing in me, my vision, and most importantly, for the encouragement, guidance, and support in bringing it to fruition.

To Carleigh Fairchild- I will always be grateful that I was able to start the process of bringing this vision to life with you as a part of that. Getting to know you, your journey, and the incredible woman that you are, was a gift that was so powerful and inspiring. I have no doubt the impact that you will have in so many lives as you go forward in sharing your story and talents with the world and all those around you.

Made in the USA
Middletown, DE
07 November 2021